bout this book

ıl advice that will be an
ng baby boomers who are
˙ement becomes a major

Gary W. Small M.D.
Director of UCLA Center on Aging
Parlow-Solomon Professor on Aging
Professor of Psychiatry and Biobehavioral Sciences

*   *   *   *

*The book **Active-Retirement** was useful for me, as I am nearing retirement. Using this journal-like handbook to walk myself through what my particular retirement can be, I let Peter Silton take my hand, ever so gently and yet securely, and willingly guide me to fill in the brief but illuminating questionnaire and move along a fascinating path. There were no "wrong" answers, no judgments--merely playing the game of life after retirement. I developed a clearer picture of a new definition of retirement--actively fulfilling the arenas of travel, expanding my musical interests and involving myself in community activities. Finally I found the guide to prioritize the lifelong dreams and how to make them happen.*

Judith Farber
Landscape Designer

*   *   *   *

Even for those not quite at retirement age, Peter Silton's book offers a wonderful blueprint for a stage of life most of us ignore until it is upon us. Furthermore, it provides genuine hope that the active and restless among us do not need to fear retirement. From the sound of it, we might even enjoy it more than our current workaholic lives! This book turns the potentially bleak into the joyous with marvelous ease, mixing philosophical and practical directions at every turn.

Michael Gitlin,
Professor of Psychiatry, UCLA School of Medicine

*   *

Active-Retirement views senior years as a new beginning, Kaneka *(rebirth)*, a time for discovering the Ken-Tao *(new life path)* within and making dreams of the spirit come true. You've been working, raising children and accumulating talents and desires. Now, you have the time and money to expand your talents and pursue your desires. Step by step, Silton's book helps you find the activities, the meaning and the support to surprise yourself with the very special Ken-Tao for the years yet to come.

Jane A. Stewart Ph.D.
Psychologist

*   *   *   *

Active-Retirement for Affluent Workaholics is a much-needed literary gem amidst an aging-energetic world. Peter Silton has skillfully penned a pragmatic and strategic operating manual for those that have passed their 50th. His optimism and creativity encourage our curiosity and interests and help us develop new goals and priorities.

Timothy J. Hayes M.D. MPH (Geriatrics)
UCLA School of Medicine

*   *   *   *

Peter Silton's book is filled with insights, practical suggestions and steps for addressing the fear of retirement. Silton shows that retirement is a beginning, not an end, a start of a phase of your life that can be every bit as active and fulfilling as your former career.

Ken Abel
Senior Management Consultant

*   *   *   *

Active-Retirement

For

Affluent Workaholics

Planning for the Life
You've Always Wanted

By Peter Silton

N.P. Financial Publishing
Los Angeles, California

Active-Retirement for Affluent Workaholics

Planning for the Life You've Always Wanted

By Peter Silton

Published by:

N.P. Financials

P.O. Box 49891
Los Angeles, CA 90049 U.S.A.
Phone-FAX: (310) 471-1353
e-Mail npfinancial@earthlink.net

Library of Congress Control Number: 200111 6263

ISBN # 1-882758-07-2

*   *   *   *   *   *   *   *   *

Disclaimer:

Contents

Acknowledgment

No book is ever the result of the author's effort alone. Many friends and professionals helped me formulate and test some of the concepts in this book. The impetus for this book came from my friend, Dr. Joel Yager, who challenged me to write about my wonderful active-retirement. I thought about it for a few days, came up with the title and the rest was only hard work.

The information I received from the numerous people I interviewed helped me to develop the theme of this book and gave me insight into the retirement process. I especially want to thank the members of the Over the Hill Gang (a group of senior skiers) and the Plato Society (an intellectual society for seniors) for their encouragement and time.

As for the actual writing, I spent many years in the computer field and have been accused of writing in computer code. For the translation of "computer code" to English I want to give special thanks to Larra Anderson. As for punctuation and structure, without an editor I would write each chapter as a single sentence. I therefore want to thank Kelly Schwartz for her commas, semicolons, and especially periods.

And to my daughter Petra Silton who did the final edit, was a wonderful critic, and demonstrated that the money I spent on her education was definitely not wasted.

And most importantly, I wish to thank Dr. Bonnie Sturner, my wife and my best friend, who challenges and inspires. I cherish our life of Active-Retirement together.

You don't get to choose how you're going to die
Or when.
You can only decide how you are going to live. Now.
Joan Baez

I dedicate this book to my wife, our five children and our wonderful friends who have participated and suffered through my experimenting in Active-Retirement.

And to all the people that did yesterday what they thought they wanted to do tomorrow.

Preface

Today Americans to live longer and healthier lives. The average age for retirement is fifty-eight. After which you can expect to live twenty or thirty years. To live those years to there fullest you need to create a plan, which deals not only with finances, but also pursuits and goals. Active-Retiring is a complex process. It means a change in lifestyle, financial needs and resources, relationships, and your life goals.

When I started my retirement at the age of 59, I had no idea what I was "really" going to do. At the time I decided to Actively-Retire, I was the owner of a software business with offices in Los Angeles and New York.

Since then I have written two books on computers and education, consulted and developed business plans for computer firms, taught entrepreneurial skills in Russia, and helped my son raise capital and structure a software business.

I also started an after-school computer class for low-income kids, and developed a technology plan and educational curriculum for a public elementary school where twenty percent of the student body consists of children of homeless. In addition I have traveled to 22 different countries, including little explored lands such as Suluwasi, Bhutan, and Nepal. And I ski twenty-five days a year.

As I began my retirement I reviewed all the things I had tried to do, all the things I wanted to do and all of the things I had done, and then made an active retirement plan.

Drawing on my own experience and interviews with members of the *Over the Hill Gang*, *The Plato Society* and friends, I have put together a book that can help anyone in the transition from work to an exciting life after retirement.

In *Active-Retirement for Affluent Workaholics*, I covered many of the areas of retirement, not as a complete encyclopedia but as a guide to the concepts of retirement. I have also included many resources for additional information. The rest is up to you. Start your journey!

1 | Wake Up Call!
If You Get Up One Morning and Don't Want to Go to Work (or You Are Just Ready to Retire)

Retirement is the ugliest word in the language.
~ Ernest Hemingway ~

Today is the first day of your life
~ Joan Baez ~

It Comes to *All* of Us

Perhaps, under the guise of a good and satisfying life, you're beginning to have a gnawing sense of missing out on something. You've accomplished everything you've set out to do in life, but you're still feeling like you want something more.

Or perhaps your company just gave you a Timex, and although you agree that it's the right time to go, your head is still buzzing with good ideas.

Or perhaps your downsizing company just offered you a "golden parachute." You don't feel like starting over someplace else, but you certainly aren't ready to sit in the den all day.

Or maybe you have been planning for retirement all along and the moment has now arrived: you have the money and the golf clubs, but unfortunately you also have a growing suspicion that retirement isn't going to work[1] for you.

Then it's time to read this book. You are a perfect candidate for Active-Retirement.

Retire? Me?!

Perhaps retirement seems inconceivable to you or is something you're hoping won't happen till the very distant future (though having a stroke at 90 does *not* count as retirement). However,

- If you've reached the point where work no longer seems as interesting as it once did
- If you have to work too hard to keep up with the young technocrats and MBAs
- Or, if you simply think there must be more to life than *this*...

---

1 Pun intended.

Then now **is** the right time to read this book. It's true, you probably won't ever be retirement material (what workaholic is?), but that doesn't mean you aren't Active-Retirement material. Maybe the children have left the nest and now need only minimum maintenance[2] and so your mind has begun to wander. Maybe you just feel ready for something else – another career, a new direction, a change of pace. If so, you are already considering a life restructuring. You might not be inclined to call it "retirement," but even if it leads to a new career in the end, it is at least a "retirement" from the life you have led for so long. It is still going to be a rebirth of some kind. And that is what Active-Retirement is all about.

So if you are an affluent workaholic who finds him or herself at any of these places in life, this book was written for you. Read on –the labor pains of your rebirth may have already begun.

How Do I Know If I'm an "Affluent Workaholic"?

You picked up this book, didn't you? But just to be sure, and because it is always a good idea to define one's terms, I'll break it down for you.

---

2 Children, even grown ones, always need maintenance.

Affluence

The freedom to do whatever you want to do – travel, write, paint, volunteer, or a number of other things that we'll be exploring together. It is having enough money to feel comfortable about spending some of it.[3] Being a mathematician by training, I itch to give you an exact figure, but it would be wrong. There is no number that's correct for everyone. What some people would consider to be an affluent sum would be insufficient for others. My advice would be to talk to a good financial advisor and obtain the numbers that would allow you to live a good life for the rest of your life. If you realize you have already achieved that goal and don't need to work for money anymore, congratulations are in order – you are affluent![4]

Workaholic

Someone who has used skill and talent to achieve identity and well being through work, while managing to successfully provide for his or her own needs and probably those of a family. In a word – you.

However, through necessity or desire (or both), your situation is about to radically change, if it hasn't already. You are about to be "freed" from that well-known identity. Free to take up a new one instead – one in which you will be able to use the things you have accumulated – the money, expertise, and caring – to explore your innermost desires and find new connections to yourself and to work.

Notice that I did not say, "you will stop working" or "you will change careers" or even mention the word "retirement." That concept of "not retiring" is a mental attitude that runs through the book and that you should try to foster as well. I acknowledge that you are a workaholic (I am as well), and so I would never ask you to stop working. But what I will ask is that you now make your work the fulfillment of your life's dreams.

---

3 If you know you have enough, but still don't feel comfortable spending it, you'll feel better after you get through Chapter 4.
4 That said, some of the most important aspects of an excellent Active-Retirement are good health, strong family relationships, and ongoing friends.

"So Who Are YOU?"

Although I have interviewed many people who were either already Actively Retired or ready to start Active Retirement, most of the concepts presented here have come from my own experiences, those of my wife, and those of an extensive circle of professional friends – all of whom are of the type assumed in this book – affluent workaholics.

You will find as you read this book that certain of my prejudices will show. I make no apologies for them. They are real, built up over many years, and cannot be easily expunged. Some of the more obvious ones are: I love skiing, I hate golf, and I'm scared to bungee jump.

But who is the person behind these nefarious biases? I'm a man in his mid-sixties who has been Actively-Retired for about ten years. Before that, my career path varied widely. After getting a B.S. in mathematics, I worked in apparel manufacturing, real estate development, and as the owner of a software and service bureau business with offices in Los Angeles, New York, and Montreal. Then came the day ten years ago when I sold my business to my employees and started out on my Active-Retirement. My wife, Bonnie, is a few years younger (I'm not allowed to give her exact age) and is a practicing psychologist on the clinical faculty at UCLA. She also maintains a private practice. Presently, she is still working, but she is rapidly being moved (she would say pushed) toward Active-Retirement.

"So What's This Book Really About?"

Since you've already read this far and not sent the book back to Amazon.com, perhaps I should give you a preview of what the rest of the book is **not** about, so you won't be disappointed:

- It is not about the best places to retire.
- It is not about retirement communities.
- It is not about what vitamins to take to keep healthy.
- It is not about estate planning.
- It is not about financial planning.
- It is not about how to retire on $20,000 a year.

It is about living an extremely full and meaningful life. It is about making a major transition into one of the most fulfilling periods of your life and ensuring that the transition is a smooth one. It is about believing that this is not done by mere number crunching and studying mutual fund ratings but by your deciding on how *you really want to live* the rest of your life.

"What Is Active-Retirement?"

What is **your** idea of retirement? Do you envision a time of leisure, playing golf, "catching up," or something else.

Below, write your definition of retirement:

My Definition of "Retirement";

_____

_____

_____

_____

_____

Does your idea sound like an "active" retirement? Or does Active-Retirement not even make sense to you? Perhaps it sounds like an oxymoron: either you are active or you are retired.

In the 21st century there are new rules for everything. The concept of your "retired years" that you grew up with simply no longer exists. You will probably live longer, healthier, and more actively than your parents. Instead of a rocking chair you will probably have a Porsche; in place of knitting you will paint, sculpt, or run a 10K race. You won't simply visit your grandchildren across town, you'll invite them to jet with you to New York, London, or Aspen to enjoy a vacation together. The actions are new, the premises are different, and the time is now!

New Words for New Ideas

English is not a very exact language. The same word can have drastically different connotations for different people. To some, "retirement" means a gold watch, time with the grandchildren, and rocking into the sunset like a Norman Rockwell painting. For Senator John Glenn, retirement meant finally having enough free time to go back into space.

Although science and business are constantly inventing new words, such as Xerox, digital, cell-phone, and e-mail, the English language is not as quick to develop modern words for states of mind or life passages. Therefore, I turned to the ancient Chinese and the wisdom of Confucius to give us (non-convoluted) words for the key concepts behind Active-Retirement.

"Kaneka"[5]

"A Rebirth." In Ancient China, when one reached the age of 5 x 12 (60), a "Kaneka" celebration was held, during which the birthday "child" was given new baby clothes to symbolize his rebirth into a second childhood. It was a rebirth of freedom, joy, play, and creativity. For us, Kaneka will mean much the same thing (though you won't have to be 60 to have one). It is the transition, the rebirth, from your old life as income earner to your new life – as a "Wenjen."

"Wenjen" (wun'jren)

"The Cultured Person." In ancient China, Wenjens were considered a special and noble class of people who not only had the affluence and freedom to pursue the life of "culture" (as opposed to working for money or the state) but also were enlightened enough to actually do it! For us, becoming a Wenjen is the end goal of the Kaneka transition: to become enlightened enough to use our working hours to pursue our heart's truest interests and desires.

"Chen-Tao" (chen' dow)

"The Correct or Right Path." There is no absolute right path, but there is a path that is right for you. What makes it "right" is how well it reflects a correct understanding of your roles and responsibilities in life, and how well it allows you to act in accord with them. By "walking this path," you will find yourself in balance and accord with the Tao (or "Truth").

---

5 Kaneka is a Japanese word for this Ancient Chinese concept.

We have already determined that your present Chen-Tao is no longer appropriate or correct for you. This is because you are coming to a point in life when your roles and responsibilities are rapidly changing. Fortunately, through your Kaneka, you can and will define new ones for yourself. And once your Kaneka is complete, and your new roles and responsibilities are defined, you will be able to clearly see and follow a new Chen-Tao – a life path that is correct and appropriate for the new heart-centered life you shall be leading.

Defining Active-Retirement

Understanding and following your new Chen-Tao is what Active-Retirement is all about. It is about living the rest of your life in the best possible way – the best way, as determined simply by who you are and what you want out of life. It is the walking of a life path that is determined by your dreams, deep-felt desires, and long-time joys – whatever those may be.

The Tools of Kaneka

The next step toward a thrilling Active-Retirement is to officially begin your Kaneka. To do so, you will need a few simple tools: an open mind and heart, enthusiasm, this book, a simple notebook, and Internet access.

This Book

The book is divided into four sections, each of which will help you successfully move through your Kaneka into a satisfying Active-Retirement.

Section I – Help: Functions as a workbook to guide you through the initial stages of your Kaneka. Here you will develop a new Chen-Tao (right path) for the next exciting phase of your life.

Section II – Making It Happen: Addresses how to achieve some of the specific goals you might have set in Section I. Feel free to pick and choose among the chapters in this section according to your interests.

Section III – Necessities: Describes the essentials for every Active-Retiree. Everyone should read these chapters.

Section IV – Resources and Information: lists all of the Web sites referenced throughout the book, in one handy chapter.

A Notebook

Yes, there will be writing exercises. They are there to open your mind to new ideas and experiences – not taken from the air, or some of the fantasies of a James Bond movie – but developed from the solid foundation of – you. So purchase a notebook and keep it with you, as you'll find that answers to questions or new goals will come to you at the oddest times.

And I do mean a paper notebook. I have tried electronic organizers and handheld computers, and although I do use them for appointments and addresses, they are not adequate for the type of journal you will be doing here. You, of course, might be thinking, "But I'm not a writer, so I don't need to do that." Or, "I don't write. I dictate." Or, "I write with a word processor." The main purpose of this journal is to allow your subconscious the opportunity to participate in your Kaneka unfettered by your rational, practical mind. Writing on paper allows your subconscious more direct and more frequent (unless you carry that word-processor with you everywhere) access to your conscious mind. Furthermore, the very structure of having all of your writing in one book allows your eyes to glance over many entries at each sitting, thereby allowing you to make even more vital connections each time you open the book to write. Lastly, something personal exists in the mind-paper-pen-letters-word relationship that doesn't exist between computers and us (at least not until they implant a microchip in our brain).

So get a notebook and divide it into two equal parts, for there are two types of writing I would like you to do.

The Kaneka Journal

The first half of your notebook will serve as your Kaneka Journal, a repository for your daily writings. This idea springs from Julia Cameron and Mark Bryan's "Morning Pages," from their book *The Artist's Way,* but here it has been tailored to meet your Kaneka needs.

During the time you are working on this book, I would like you to write one page in your Kaneka Journal first thing in the morning, every morning. Handwrite this page in your notebook, do it quickly, continuously, and without self-editing, until the page is full.

Before each writing session, start with the intention, "What are my heart's truest desires?" Then just write. Write about whatever comes into your head. It doesn't matter if it is a page of gripes, or simply the description of the dream you haven't gotten out of your head yet, or the list of things you need to do that came crowding into your mind the moment you woke up. Whatever it is – write it down. Initially, it might not seem connected to your elevated intention, but slowly you will begin to see the connections.

As you empty and clear your mind this way each morning, you may realize that the images you are writing down from your dream are of Arabia – and that you have always wanted to travel there. You may find that your list of gripes generates the steam you needed to change what's been frustrating you and bring you closer to your real desires. It may suddenly occur to you, as you list your daily to-do's, that you could hire someone to do all that boring stuff for you, so that you can get on to the good stuff in life. As you write, let whatever comes out of your mind, come out – and watch for the pearls of wisdom it brings with it.

For the first three weeks, *don't go back* or read over anything you have already written. Just dump out everything that comes to mind every morning for three weeks, and move on. This will allow your subconscious mind time to express itself without fearing that the conscious mind will come in and edit or judge it. Your subconscious behaves like a shy informant. Look over its shoulder too often and it will hide the good stuff. But let it go and give it a little time to build up some steam and it will reward you with bigger and better gems every day.

After three weeks, schedule an hour to read over the pages you have written (at least twenty-one, because you wrote every day, didn't you?). Then, spend another twenty minutes "taking stock." Write out any themes, ideas, desires, or issues that came out in those pages that you think are particularly important to you or that you want to remember. When you are done, dog-ear this page (or use a fancy metal page point if you are so disposed). As you go along, these dog-ears will become your quick reference to the pages where your distilled thoughts lie. You will find yourself going back to them again and again during your Kaneka.

Begin another three weeks of daily pages, uninterrupted by any rereading or self-editing. At the end of the three weeks, take stock once again. Continue this process throughout your Kaneka.

Fill in the Blank

As you read through the chapters of this book there will be questions to answer, ideas to brainstorm, and lists to formulate. Use the second half of your notebook for these exercises.[6] Some of these exercises I developed on my own and some came from books that resonated either with me or with others during our Kanekas. Regardless of where the exercises originated, I suggest you give them all a serious try. The ideas that are borrowed are footnoted with the title and author of the original book. If one of these ideas particularly resonates with you, take a look at the book from which it originated, for these books can help you with your Kaneka as well.

Internet Access

The Internet is going to be a crucial resource for your Kaneka and all along your new Chen-Tao. As you read these chapters you will find numerous suggested Web sites and opportunities for Internet research. A complete listing by topic of all of these Web sites can also be found in Chapter 14: "Web Sites for Wenjens."

If you don't already have a computer with Internet access, or if you do not know how to use a computer or access the Internet – please skip to Chapter 13 for a few thoughts on the matter.

Summing Up

You are an affluent workaholic who has walked along the same life path for many years. But now you're coming to a fork in the road, and instead of settling for retirement, you have chosen to take on Active-Retirement and the joyful life that it **will** bring. To this end, I suggest the following:

1. Realize that you are "retiring" from your old path in order to embark on a vital, highly active new one.
2. Remember that you are affluent enough to stop working for money (and to even spend some)!

---

6 Many exercises will require the notebook for your answers, but I have also left space in the book for your answers. Feel free to write them where you choose.

3. Know that just because you are "retiring" doesn't mean you are not working; rather, **Active-Retirement** means you will be working in pursuit of your heart-driven goals.

4. Consider that your idea of retirement is probably outdated and that the world it was created for doesn't exist any longer.

5. Now, replace this idea with the new concept of becoming a Wenjen (the affluent and enlightened individual who spends his "work" time pursuing his own goals, not just income) through participating in a Kaneka (rebirth) that will create a new Chen-Tao (Correct Path) for his life.

6. Then, get a notebook. Commit to writing one page in your Kaneka Journal daily, using the intention, "What are my heart's truest desires?"

7. Do not reread any of these pages for three weeks. Then take an accounting of their most important ideas and compile them on a "taking stock" page. Dog-ear the page. Repeat this process every three weeks.

8. Commit to doing the other writing exercises as they come up.

9. Now get cracking on the rest of the book! You have a Kaneka to do!

I always knew that one day
I would take this road, but yesterday
I did not know today would be the day.
~ Unknown ~

The art of progress is to preserve order amid change and to
preserve change amid order.
~ Alfred North Whitehead ~

Although retirement traditionally doesn't occur until age 65, I am sure that your attitude hasn't been, "Okay, so I'll just wait until then to think about it." By this time in your life you have probably prepared for this eventuality – financially.

However, how much time have you put into preparing for this change in other areas of your life? Finances aren't the only aspect of your life affected when you step away from a career. The affects of this change can also have profound ramifications in your personal, social, and familial arenas.

Before you begin your Kaneka,1 you will need to adequately prepare for retirement with more than just pension plans or IRAs. Unless you adequately plan for how this transition will affect your personal life, you may one day suffer from "retirement shock," a psychological condition that results from being totally emotionally unprepared for retirement. Fortunately, you still have time to prepare – but just as you planned financial retirement, you should plan for the other aspects of your retirement.

Leaving Your Job – And Its Related Issues

If it was as simple as just "stopping work," there would be no need for this chapter, but this transition is going to be a major shift in your life.

For most of your life, your work has taken the majority of your thought, time, and energy. Even if you managed to make other things a higher priority emotionally (which as a workaholic may have been quite

---

1 "Kaneka" is a rebirth into Active-Retirement (traditionally taking place at age 60).

a challenge), simply by virtue of the time and effort it takes, your work has played a significant role in your daily life. As a result, your work has ramifications in your life stream that go far beyond the earning of money. The particulars may be different for each person, but the general ideas remain the same. See if any of the following statements apply to you:

"I get most of my daily sense of self-satisfaction from my activities and accomplishments at work."

Some of the specific daily benefits I get are (circle the ones that fit you):

- creative satisfaction

- intellectual satisfaction

- sense of accomplishment

- the joy of problem solving

- the satisfaction of effectively managing others

- praise for a job well done

- enjoyment of a healthy sense of competition

- the satisfaction of successfully teaming or interacting with others

Fill in any others that apply to you:

- _____

- _____

- _____

"I define myself as the person I am at work."

Fill in your "titles" below. You may identify yourself in terms of your title, for example, as "John/Jane Smith, Vice President of Procurement for AMMC (A Major Multinational Company)," but you may also be "the problem solver," "the top salesperson," "the financial genius," "the diplomat," or "the boss." Fill in all of the various titles you will be losing when you stop your current job:

- _____
- _____
- _____
- _____
- _____

"Most of my friends and the people I associate with are somehow related to my work."

Sometimes this fact is not evident right off the bat. People have been your friends or associates for years, and you no longer think of them as simply "work"-related relationships. However, many social relationships are still based on work experiences. Below, list the people you (and your partner) socialize with. Then put a check next to those people with whom you have a career/work connection:

Name(s)	Work?
• _____	_____
• _____	_____
• _____	_____
• _____	_____

- _____ _____
- _____ _____
- _____ _____
- _____ _____

"Most of my 'social' activities are work related or with work-related people."

Many times the people we socialize with determine the activities we do in our off-hours. If there are any activities that you regularly participate in that are work related or done with work-related people, list them here. Review your list and consider how often you would do these activities if it weren't for work or work-related connections. Write "=" next to those you would still do just as much, "+" next to those you would do more, "–" next to those you would do less, and "0" next to those you wouldn't do at all.

Activity	How often?
_____	_____
_____	_____
_____	_____
_____	_____
_____	_____

"At social gatherings, I spend a lot of time talking about work or work-related issues, activities, or people."

Some people love to talk shop, while others avoid it like the plague. Even if you are one of the latter, the people we socialize with still determine what we discuss in their company. Below, list the topics of conversation you tend to participate in at dinners, events, or social gatherings. Then put a check next to those you would not discuss (or discuss significantly less) if you eliminated your present work or any of the people or activities you are connected to through work. Remember the hidden connections: If you only discuss jazz with Laura and Brian – that counts as work related if Laura is a work associate; and if you only play golf as an extension of work, you won't be discussing your most recent forays at the neighborhood cocktail party once you retire:

Topic of Conversation   Work?

- _____   _____

- _____   _____

- _____   _____

- _____   _____

- _____   _____

- _____   _____

- _____   _____

- _____   _____

Wow – This Change Is Going to Be HUGE!

Yes it is – but it doesn't have to feel that way. Not if you start developing areas of your life outside your normal work routine now, **before** you begin Active-Retirement.

Nurture Outside Interests

You probably have hobbies, charities, sports, intellectual activities, or even other business interests outside work. You might have every intention of continuing or even expanding upon these interests during your active retirement. If you have not decided whether you will want to continue any of these activities, now would be the time to do so. Just remember, an activity is not like a mountain – just because it's there doesn't mean you have to climb it.

If, after thinking about your current activities, you decide there aren't really any that you would want to continue or expand upon after you stop working, then it is important to begin developing new interests **now** – before you quit work.

The outside interests that you nurture now and continue to enjoy after you leave your job will be the ones that will offer you the activities, topics of conversation, self-satisfaction, and sense of achievement that will endure well into your retirement.

These interests create a bridge between your old life and your new one and give you **needed** elements of life that should not stop just because you decided to stop putting time into your job.

Nurture Friendships Outside Work

Make and nurture friendships that are not related to work. If you already have friends in some of the outside activities that you plan on continuing after you leave work, begin to strengthen these connections. If you have not established relationships outside work extend yourself to people who are interested in areas that you want to be involved in during Active-Retirement. For example, if you plan to take up skydiving, the following new friends could be important:

- An insurance agent who doesn't ask too many questions about hobbies.
- A chiropractor who specializes in body realignment after landing (on foot) at 50 mph.
- Someone who actually does skydiving.

Another reason to nurture new friendships is that your schedule is going to change after you leave work. You will have time to pursue some of your present interests, such as hiking, in the middle of the week or perhaps extend your travel periods. Perhaps your present buddies won't be Kaneka-ing at exactly the same time as you, or perhaps theirs will take them in different directions. Joining groups that center on activities you want to pursue during Active-Retirement will give you connections with people who may be free to go sailing with you on Tuesdays or who'd like to go skiing once every month.

Begin to Look for Self-Worth Outside Work

One of the most difficult parts of the transition certainly can be the change in your self-view and self-esteem. Your first day alone in the house is not the best time to come up with a list of interesting things you still like about yourself.

Before that day arrives, try to define yourself in new ways – by your inherent qualities or by your involvement in new interests. Even if you were "Senior Executive Vice-President," isn't it just as exciting to say "World Traveler," "Painter," "Writer," "Renaissance Man/Woman," or "Bungee Jumping Enthusiast" (and perhaps at this point, maybe even a bit more exciting)?

At social gatherings, try out new topics of discussion. Politics, books, travel, philosophy, and literature are worthy alternatives to talking about work. Yes, you might find that you are not talking to the same people at the party – but you also might find this a welcome change. Maybe you'll find a friend in someone who had been an acquaintance before. Even though you may still be working, there isn't any reason to focus on work in your "down time." You've let work occupy the center of your life long enough, and you've been very successful at it – so successful that you can afford to let your thoughts expand to other areas now.

Moving into the Home: Expectations and Negotiations

Another neglected facet of the transition away from work is the move into the home. This isn't just building a home office to shield you from non-Kaneka-ing members of the household. It is a matter of communicating with all of your family about what they can expect in your post-work life and what you will be doing.

You will soon be entering a world where your time and finances are entirely different from what they have been. This change probably does not only affect you. I can assure you that your partner, your family, and even your friends and associates all have certain expectations of how your new situation will affect **them**. Although you may have your own expectations, the key is to make sure everyone is on the same page – before retirement actually starts.

Oh, So Much Time!

Some of the transitions you will make relate to how you spend your time and redefining your role at home. Even if you do not have a partner, other family members and friends might have expectations of how you should spend what they see as "free" time. Your expectations and theirs might not match up. That is why it is very important that these issues be discussed, understood, and, if necessary, negotiated far in advance of the first Monday in twenty years that you get to sleep in past 6 AM.

If you are partnered, begin a communication and negotiation process with your partner. The most important step in that process is the communication. Each of you needs to express your expectations, especially about how you plan to participate in the other's activities after your work has ended. These expectations might be radically different. The following is an example of some private thoughts of partners when a "worker of the house" is planning on retirement (gender is arbitrary):

Chris: "Now I can watch the Angels play! And go deep-sea fishing! I can read all the Judith Krantz novels!"

Toby: "Now the stove can finally be repaired... And the garage can finally be cleaned... and the bedroom painted... and..."

Compromise: Purchase a portable television so that baseball can be watched while the garage is cleaned and the bedroom painted.

Anyway, you get the idea. The topic of what to do with your time needs to be discussed. The sharing of duties, the trips and projects done as a couple, as well as the solo expeditions should all be put on the table.

Some of the couples I interviewed planned on traveling together. Others took trips separately to pursue their own activities, such as orchid collecting, trekking, or skiing, because their partners did not have the time, interest, or physical abilities to undertake that type of trip. The most important part of making your plans is that they be discussed (not announced) and then agreed to. A pronouncement that you are going on a two-month trip to Egypt to dig up mummies, when your partner thinks you should be painting the bedroom, can put you under a curse before you even leave home.

After your partner comes everyone else. Determine how much time you currently spend with your family (including children, grandchildren, and other relatives). Then, consider whether you'd like this amount to change after retirement. Now consider how much time you think you will want to spend with key friends. As always, **before** you start disappointing or imposing on anyone, open discussions with your family and then your friends about your desires and expectations and see how your expectations match up with theirs. This will give everyone a chance to negotiate a comfortable and satisfactory schedule before your son's family is disappointed that you chose to go to Rome for Christmas this year instead of hosting the annual gathering, or your daughter begins to worry that your visits are going to become weekly, or your best friends get their hopes crushed when they find out that you do not want to do all your future traveling as a unit.

Oh, So Much Cash

Upon retirement you might get a lump sum payout or have sudden access to your entire retirement fund. This can fuel (or create) the desire to buy a few things. If you have a partner, it is crucial that any new purchases be negotiated – **ahead of time**.

The "tools" for retirement you **think you must have may not be your partner's idea of the necessities of life.**

This scene, like the others, is fictional. Any resemblance to living characters is strictly accidental.

Chris: "I'd like new curtains for the bedroom, a new set of golf clubs, and that super-light fishing gear."

Toby: "That Gucci travel bag, those pink patent leather stilettos, and a set of parabolic skis are a must."

Get together and make sure that you agree on a budget first and foremost. Then develop and negotiate any special spending plans. Finally, make sure that each of you has discretionary funds for "necessary" items (that your partner thinks are frivolous).

There is no plan that works for every couple. You have to work out your own dynamics. However, my suggestion is not to make your money plan too tight – after all, you are affluent and you don't have to account for every nickel and dime.

An Aside About Cash Flow

Many adjustments will need to be made during your Kaneka. Therefore, keep as many things as stable as possible. One of the most difficult adjustments to make is a change in cash flow (money coming in), but it doesn't need to be that way. To keep my financial balance, I arranged with my money managers, Schwab, to send me a monthly check for exactly the same amount as my previous salary. Payments began on schedule immediately after my last day at work. This meant that there was no interruption in cash flow. This type of arrangement can be made through your bank or brokerage house and can provide a much smoother transition for your entire household.

Start NOW!

You have one of the most important tools for your transition right in your hands. Don't wait until you retire to work on this book. The further you get in the activities and exercises in this book before you leave the office, the more seamless the transition will be. Instead of having a sinking feeling of "what will I do," you will count off the days with the restless, excited feeling of "I can't wait!"

So begin your Kaneka Journal now and get through (at least!) the first five chapters before you "retire." The work of planning your Kaneka is going to be so exciting that I assure you won't run out of things to do or ideas to stimulate you before you start packing up that office.

Give Yourself a Break

Finally, accept that the transfer will not take place overnight. Nor will it be entirely without bumps. You have years of habits built up from this work life of yours (and your partner does, too). So accept that your Kaneka will take some time. The main thing you can do is to make sure that you have new interests, plans, goals, and intentions already in place so that you don't wake up one morning and have no place to rush off to. For a workaholic, that would not be any fun.

Summing Up

Before you leave work you must prepare for the magnificent transformation your life is about to undergo. Financial preparation is not enough. To have a successful Kaneka you need to begin preparing the other areas of your life that will be affected by your leaving work. To this end, I suggest the following:

1. Acknowledge in what ways your work gives you a daily sense of self-satisfaction.
2. Identify the ways in which you define yourself by your work.
3. Identify which of your friends and associates are work related.
4. Identify which common activities are work related and decide how interested you are in continuing these activities after you leave your job. Identify topics of conversation you participate in at social gatherings that are work related in some way.
5. Review your outside interests. Decide which you want to continue after you leave your job.
6. Begin to develop friendships with people outside work – especially with people who might share an outside interest.
7. Begin to define yourself by outside interests and/or accomplishments other than work.
8. In social environments, try discussing outside interests rather than talking shop.
9. At home, clearly communicate and negotiate with your partner about expectations for both time and expenditures. (And set up a system so that cash flow is not interrupted.)
10. With family and friends, do the same.
11. Start implementing all of these preparations *now* – in advance of your Kaneka. Use this book as a key tool and get through the first five chapters before you "retire."
12. Be patient with yourself! Change takes time!

To be able to fill leisure intelligently
is the last product of civilization.
~ Arnold Toynbee ~

You wake up one morning and find that after years of always needing more of it, you are suddenly rich with time. Miles and miles of time. So much time that it may feel a bit uncomfortable. But you are an active and intelligent person, so you know you will do something "constructive" with it. But what exactly, you may not be entirely sure.

Like all resources, the gift of time deserves some careful planning of its investment. Your time is too precious a commodity to be spent frivolously or without some real forethought. So take the time to plan things out. You will find that a little careful consideration and planning can make your investment pay off in huge dividends of satisfaction and fulfillment.

New Ideas and Goals

We all know how easy it is to "fill up" time (chores naturally expand to fill up whatever free time one has), but filling time up is not what we are talking about here. We are **not** referring to all the yard work you finally have the time to complete (unless, of course, your true passion is landscape design). We are talking about a Kaneka – your participation in an active transition into an energetic and expansive stage of life!

In order to achieve your Kaneka, you will first need to develop a new life path. Paths are necessary through each of life's stages, and you are about to transition into your newest stage. For years now your job (or jobs) and family have given you a clear-cut path to follow. You have now reached a very privileged time in life – a time when you get to actually choose your own path.

It is the privilege of all the years of hard work and the experience gained. It is a privilege that takes careful consideration, for it gives you the rare opportunity to step back and choose your next path through life with total freedom.

"Total freedom?!?" you say. "I don't have total freedom! I have a partner, and children, and grandchildren, a house (or two), finances (My God – estate planning!), thousands of loose ends from years of never having time, and then there is still all that yard work!"

WHOA! Breathe! Let's just step back from being beleaguered by everything that already exists, and consider for a moment all that doesn't. Instead of focusing on all the paths that you have already taken (and that still seem to pull at you), let's think for a moment about all the paths that you have not taken.

Paths Not Taken[1]

At each step in your life, at each turning point or fork in the road, you made a decision. You made it for some cognitive, emotional, or other reason, but you chose a direction in which to go. That means at every fork in the road, there was another branch that you did not follow. Let's take a moment to consider those other paths. Take the time (it

---

1 From an idea by Ira Progoff in his At a Journal Workshop. (1975)

won't hurt – you have plenty) and consider a moment. What did you really want to be when you were six:

_____

twelve? _____

sixteen? _____

twenty? _____

twenty-four? _____

twenty-eight? _____

Now, you're the only one who knows how old you were that day you had that really strong craving to quit your job and join the Merchant Marines, so you fill in the blanks from now on:

At _____ I wanted to _____

At _____ I wanted to _____

At _____ I wanted to _____

Did it always stay the same? Did you really always want to be a dentist, or did you want to be a jazz musician at some point? Okay, so even if dentistry always was your one true calling, surely at some point you felt the tug of adventure other than the impacted root canal. Did you want to sail the world in a one-person sailboat? Did you want to paint the French coast? Did you want to trek in Tibet? Afghanistan? New England? It doesn't matter if your idea of the world's greatest exploit was simply sitting in a high- backed chair and reading all the great books one by one – just as long as you know what adventures appealed to you in the past. List them right now:

1. I always wanted to _____

_____

2.   There was that time I thought I wanted to   _____

_____

3.   I always thought it would be neat to   _____

_____

4   If my life had been very different, I always imagined I   '

might/could have   _____

_____

5.   I couldn't see myself doing it, but I think   _____

_____

would be an amazing experience for someone to have.

Try one in your own words:

6.   _____

_____

No adventure is too "silly" or difficult to consider. Even the idea of your bungee jumping over the Victoria Falls isn't so silly that it can't be written down. You've certainly managed more challenging things in your life, this is just a list on paper, and you don't have to show it to anyone! So if you held some ideas back, then list them here:

7. _____

_____

8. _____

_____

Activities not done [2]

Now let us consider the smaller adventures in life. The list of things you just never had the time for but always wanted to get to: painting, walking, gardening, surfing, or actually reading the Sunday *New York Times* (which could be a full-time job – by the time you finish it, the next one arrives). This list is frustratingly easy –

What I never got/get a chance to do, but still really want to!

_____

_____

_____

_____

_____

_____

_____

2 ibid.

_____

_____

_____

_____

_____

_____

_____

I don't mean to stop you short, because I am sure you could go on for pages (and that's where your journal might come in handy): however, we are working toward something, and before we can get there, I need to bring up one more concept for you, activities done with self-satisfaction.

Activities with Self-Satisfaction [3]

Certainly over the years there have been activities you have done that have given you a grand sense of satisfaction (and I am not talking about the time you won that battle with your insurance company, although I know how good that probably felt). Whether it was snorkeling on your vacation or building Victorian — style dollhouses for each of your granddaughters at Christmas, there have been activities that just felt great to you. (So great that it didn't really matter that Sally was still more interested in her plastic Barbie Townhouse.)

Because these activities gave us so much pleasure, they are very much worthy of a list. But start out by doing us both a favor — eliminate the word selfish from your vocabulary. Anything that helps you grow and develop as an individual and gives you self-satisfaction is worthwhile. There are many things that you can do to give to the community and to people who need assistance, but there isn't any reason that these ideas need to be mutually exclusive. So first, let's identify those activities that give you satisfaction: be they sports, books, painting, or going to the best concerts and plays. Then, once we know what

_____

3 ibid.

connects us in a fulfilling way with the world, we will be in a better position to serve it.[4]

So please go ahead, relish the memories of those activities that make or have made you feel the best:

_____

_____

_____

_____

_____

_____

_____

_____

_____

_____

Your "Chen-Tao"

All right! We are just about ready to consider your path-to-be again. The path that you will choose and create through your Kaneka transition and that you will follow through your new life as a Wenjen (an enlightened, affluent person). I am talking about the Chen-Tao, or Right Path, for your next stage of life.

But what makes a particular path right for you? It might seem impossible to conceive of any one path that might fit well after having just looked at the myriad of things that you enjoy doing (or desire to do).

_____

4 You can explore how to combine activities and skills that you enjoy with charitable work in Chapter 10.

It would appear that any "right" path would have to cover all of these things.

In ancient China, it was considered a noble and honored path to dedicate oneself to the pursuit of being a "cultured" human being. By this was meant the involvement in aspects of life that was not merely for work, family, or the state but was for the enrichment of the individual himself. However this privilege was only possible for the Wenjen, because only the person who had affluence, freedom and enlightenment was in a position to pursue this path. Fortunately for you — you have affluence and freedom, (remember all that time?) — and you are becoming more enlightened by the minute!

A Wenjen follows a path that is cut and defined by his own heartfelt goals, rather than determined by other forces. That is his Chen-Tao. In other words, once you become enlightened enough to realize that your affluence gives you the freedom to pursue your own goals (trust me, keep reading and you'll get there), your very pursuit of those goals will be the walking of your Chen-Tao. You will come to realize that by just pursuing your heart-desired goals, you will be on your right and honored path through this important stage of your life. You will be a Wenjen walking your Chen Tao.

Sounds fabulous (or just fantastic)? Then you should identify those goals! Let's make another list. The Big List. The list of what is to come.

The Big List

This is a list of things you feel you really want to do. Not have to do, should do, would be good for you to do, your partner would like you to do, or you used to want to do, but "things that **You really feel you want to do.**" And **do not** let the "I really can't do that," or the "I can't afford to do that" syndrome get to you. This is just a list. Not reality. You may not be able to do certain things, that's true. However, if you figure out what you really want without limiting yourself now, then later you just might be able to find a good substitute that fulfills that original aspiration.

I suggest limiting the number of items on your list to five, at this point. If you list a hundred things you want to do you may never do any of them, but if there are under ten, the inventive mind of a true Wenjen will find a way to achieve some of them.

Actually, it may not be easy to commit to things you **really** want to do. It can require you to break down some psychological barriers (my partner will think I've gone crazy), parental no-no's (that's too dangerous, young ladies don't do that, being adult is about being responsible), and years of your path being defined by work. Is that work person *who you are*? "I'm a meat packer." End of conversation? Never mind that you've climbed Everest, written six books on Hegel, and hold the record on multiple skydives — you're a meat packer.

Break out of these holds on your dreams. This is not the time to be defined by anything other than the voices inside of you. (And they are all there – there in the lists you have already created. In your childhood dreams, your unconscious desires, and your sometimes hidden joys.) It is just means returning to those lists and deciding which desires still burn inside of you. And you know which they are. They're the ones that make your heart skip a little beat, or that warm your cheeks or that bring a little smile to your face when you read them.

Don't add any items to the Big List that merely generate a "that sounds nice, I might like to do that" or especially an "it would really be good for me to do that." **Only** add those items that get the "Boy, now **that** sounds great! I really want to do that!"

And don't take the Big List so seriously that you don't get started! Despite its big name, it's not cast in concrete, but in play dough so that it can be molded and can change as you (and your partner) change and grow as Wenjen.

So go ahead!!! Review your previous lists and then write down five things you feel you really want to do:

THE BIG LIST (Part 1)

1. _____

2. _____

3. _____

4. _____

5. _____

And so on…

_____

_____

_____

_____

_____

_____

_____

_____

_____

_____

_____

_____

_____

_____

_____

_____

If after going over all your own lists you are still feeling unsure or not fully inspired, you can pass over the lists I've compiled on the next page. There you may find a few more items to add to your own. Or perhaps something there will simply spark a good idea.

DO NOT READ MY LIST BEFORE ATTEMPTING TO MAKE YOUR OWN BIG LIST!!!!!!!!

This list is just to help you brainstorm after your own storm clouds have started to sputter out. It's a jumping off point. I've grouped the ideas by physical and intellectual activities. Don't get caught up grouping yours this way. I find when making a list it is best to stick with an open one and just let your mind wander. It brings forth ideas that may reside in your subconscious. These activities are just grouped like this to increase your reading ease.

Physical Activities
Walk the Appalachian trail
Scuba dive four times a year
Trek in New Zealand
Hike in Switzerland
Sail the Caribbean
Ski more regularly
Trek in Nepal

Learning Activities
The computer and how to access the Internet
A new language
Learn to play the piano, violin, banjo, etc.
Get a degree – BA/BS, MA, Ph.D.
How to play golf
To play chess
To fly a plane
Take up Scuba diving
Click with Photography
Jump at sky diving
Start knitting or weaving
Go sailing
Reach for yoga

Intellectual Activities
Visit the Louvre in Paris or the Uffizzi in Florence
Read the Great Books of Western Civilization
Read the Great Books of Eastern Civilization
Write nonfiction books and/or articles
Translate Haiku from the Japanese
Write a book about skiing

Study Art History in Italy

Creative Activities

Write a book of poetry
Design your dream home
Start your own business
Compose music
Design furniture
Design clothes
Write memoirs
Build furniture
Write a novel
Do modern dance
Sculpt a horse
Draw nature
Paint a portrait
Perform in a choir
Act in a play

Spiritual Activities

Spend a month at a monastery
Travel to the Holy Lands
Travel to Tibet or India
Take a vision quest
Learn to meditate
Study with a guru
Become a nun

Travel

Take a historical trip based on a time period, culture,
    historical event, or the life of a past figure
Visit opening night of the opera at La Scala
Attend the Mozart festival in Salzburg
Take a boat trip down the Amazon
Walk in the Italian Lake Country
See the New England fall color
Go on a photo safari in Africa
Live in New York for a month
Ride the Orient Express

Take a boat to Alaska
Go on a balloon ride
Go deep sea fishing
See Wimbledon

Hobbies

Build my own radio controlled plane
Become involved with local theatre
Visit the Baseball Hall of Fame
Ride all the different train lines
Attend national trading shows
Create a perennial garden
Publish a book of recipes
Become a gourmet chef
Raise pigeons
Build a kit car

Miscellaneous

I still want to join the Merchant Marines
Move to an active retirement complex
Win the lottery

One More Time!

So now that you have seen my ideas, are there any new items you would like to put down on your Big List? Perhaps these are items from my lists that made you say "Yes!" or perhaps something on my lists simply jogged your mind enough to remember a few other things you really want to do. In either case — if anything new came up, or if you still had a few ideas left over after your first five, — add them to your list now:

THE BIG LIST (Part 2)

6. _____

7. _____

8. _____

The Big List in Action

Making the Big List is part of your Kaneka. It is the first step. The next step is making it concrete.

Say What You Mean and Mean What You Say

The Big List gains efficacy when it becomes specific. So go back over it and look for anyplace where you can give it more shape. For example, your "do more traveling" could translate to "travel to London" or "travel around the world" or "travel the African continent." Or "sing" could mean, "take operatic voice lessons," or "perform on stage" or "record an album." Go over your selections and plumb your heart. When you mustered up the courage to say "learn how to sail," did you really mean "learn how to sail my own yacht around the Caribbean"? Go for it! Now is the time and place. What if it is a big project? You're old enough to have learned that even the biggest projects happen just one step at a time.

So, go over your items on the Big List (Parts 1 and 2) and make them as specific as possible. Put down your new, **specific** version of the Big List here:

THE BIG LIST (Part 3)

1. _____

   _____

2. _____

   _____

3. _____

   _____

4. _____

   _____

5. _____

_____

_____

6. _____

_____

7. _____

_____

8. _____

_____

Can I Get Tea for Two?

If you have a partner, obviously he or she will have make a separate Big List. Now is the time to ask your partner to consider writing one. Once you and your partner have prepared your own individual and specific lists, it is time to negotiate the activities with your partner. You may find that your dreams are radically different! You may want to read all the books you have never had a chance to read, while your partner may want to learn how to sky dive, which really, as long as your partner's insurance is paid up, he or she can do anything, while you are left behind to scour Plato.

There are five alternatives for the Partnered:
1. Your partner likes some items on your list and you decide to do those together.
2. Your partner doesn't really like some of the items on your list but will be a good sport and go along.
3. Your partner doesn't like some items but tells you to do them alone "if it will make you happy."
4. Your partner tells you that you are insane and shouldn't be doing all those crazy things anyhow.
5. You decide to get rid of your partner (nothing violent).

In any case, from this point on, you will need to be aware of "my," "my partner's", and "our" Big Lists if you plan on achieving successful Kaneka for both you and your partner.

If you don't have a partner, then there are other decisions you will have to make about single activities and travel. Single activities are a lot of fun and can introduce you to many new people. Activities with a friend can help keep the momentum going. Single travel opens you up to many new adventures that you might not otherwise have encountered. But travel with a friend will probably mean that you will loose that friend.

Taking the Leap

Okay. So we have now fulfilled the "what" part of your Big List. Now, in order for it to become a reality, you should tackle the question of "when." I don't believe you merely say, "I want to get up in the morning," but rather "I want to get up at 8:00 a.m." Similarly, any activity that you really want to happen, and that you have control over, should be put into a time frame. (You do not have control over winning the lottery, sorry to say). If we were to continue with our above examples, you could plan "traveling to London" for March of next year. Your new activity now reads: "traveling to London in March of next year." How about "recording an album"? Recording studios can easily be rented. You can plan a session to take place next October. It gives you plenty of time to prepare. So now this activity reads: "recording an album next October." That's good, and you'll still have plenty of time to go to London in March.

What about "learn how to sail my own yacht around the Caribbean"? Well, considering you need to learn how to sail, and acquire a yacht, and prepare it for a long trip — perhaps three years from today would be a good time frame. There isn't any reason a bigger goal like this can't still be scheduled. It just needs to be broken down into parts. All long-term goals are achieved in this way. Your scheduling simply needs to reflect each of the parts necessary to achieve your long-term goal. So perhaps you could schedule a sailing intensive over each summer for the next three years. Then schedule boat research over the first winter, boat buying (or time-sharing or renting) over the second, and boat crewing and preparation for over the last winter on shore. Then, by the beginning of that fourth year, you should be ready to go and you'll be right on schedule. Fabulous!

The Big Plan

So give it one last go — rewrite your specific Big List (Part 3), and this time write each item out as a scheduled **event** — whether it be as simple as reading that classic you've always wanted to re-read or as complex as planning a trip to Bhutan. Further possibilities could include researching archeological digs in Peru, sending off letters to various digs to volunteer your services for the following January, getting responses and deciding which dig to join by next June, and planning and preparing for your travels from then on until you fly to Peru to join the archeological dig in the Andes that February.

Now, I would give you space below in which to change your Big List "items" into Big Plan "events," but I believe you are going to need quite a lot of space to do it properly. So break out those journals we spoke of in Chapter 1 (you did get one, didn't you?) and begin. Give yourself twenty minutes and write out all eight "events" thoroughly.

It's exciting, isn't it — to be actively in the midst of your Kaneka?!

What Now?

Now is the time for you to begin to ask how, because if you don't start asking how right away, chances are very good that in April you will be saying, "Hey! Weren't we supposed to go to London last month?" Instead, now is the time to begin going over each event on your Big Plan, and to assess how you are going to accomplish it.

"Does that mean I need to start planning a trip?" Correct! Give that man/woman an umbrella for his/her upcoming trip to London. And then tell them to turn to *Chapter 9: Travel* and *Chapter 13: Computers, Research, Resources, and the Internet*. The "how" is what the rest of this book is about! How to do the research, how to manage the resources, how to find out and figure out and actually do whatever it is that you've decided you want to do. It is all possible and hopefully this book will clearly show you how.

You should be so proud! You started with a wish, gave it a touch of reality by putting a time frame on it, and now you are about to pour the concrete that will solidify your ephemeral desires. So get reading! Your flight is scheduled to leave soon and your Kaneka has already begun!

Summing Up

You are entering a time of life when your old definitions and life's path no longer work for you. But because you are a particularly active, intelligent, and affluent person, you have chosen to go through a Kaneka — to actively participate in a rebirth into a highly active and special time of life — the time of being an enlightened Wenjen.

The Wenjen's path is created by the pursuit of one's own heart's goals. In order to discover your own heart's goals and thereby begin to follow your own path through your new life, I suggest the following:

1. Identify and list any paths you chose not to take at any previous point in your life.
2. Identify adventures or pursuits that have always appealed to you.
3. Identify activities that you would like, but never have or had the time to pursue.
4. Identify past activities that gave you a real sense of satisfaction.
5. From these lists (and from the list I provided) compile a list of eight activities you still really want to pursue.
6. Make this Big List specific.
7. Schedule each item on your Big List — in detail.
8. Start planning how to accomplish each newly scheduled event, and let the rest of this book help you do it!

You don't get to choose how you die. Or when. You can only
decide how you are going to live. Now.
~ Joan Baez ~

Once you accept your own death,
all of a sudden you are free to live.
~ Saul Alinsky ~

Time, Income, Gifting, Inheritance, and Attitude

As I am sure you know all too well by now, time does equal money. In fact, isn't this the very equation that puts the panic into retirement financial planning? Suddenly there is this indeterminate stretch of time that needs to be covered by a finite amount of money. The old-fashioned idea that retirement means no more work and therefore no more income kicks right in. Images of spending one's elder years living on a carefully planned "restricted income" or of your family bogged down by your unplanned-for medical costs come crashing down on Big List hopes and dreams. Alas, it seems like reality came in and destroyed your great plans before you even got a chance to start.

No, it isn't true! This old idea has no relationship to your present situation or path. What you need is to look at the true "reality" of your post-Kaneka world. And the first step toward re-conceiving your future financial situation as one of financial flexibility is to accept a simple truth - **you have a finite amount of time before you fall off the perch**.

The negative way of looking at this is obvious. The positive, however, is that the money you have now **does not** have to last forever. It doesn't. Even though the human life span continues to lengthen, we still will not ever achieve immortality. And once you accept that fact, it brings retirement financial planning into the very finite realm.

Now I am not suggesting you follow the example of the U.S. government when it declares that Social Security will go broke in 2032 at 2:30 pm (which is pretty much nonsense considering the government can't even predict the scope of the surplus three months in advance). Even if there was a sure method of determining the exact date at which you would reach a zero balance, would knowing that your checks would begin bouncing on your 137th birthday really enliven your approach to spending today?

What is needed is an approach that simply takes reality into account. You have money. You have a limited period of time. So let's be realistic - at **the very most** how much time do you have? In the 1930s, when 65 was determined to be retirement age for Social Security, the average American only lived to 63. Today it's 75. And by the year 2040, the average American will be living longer, but only to 81. So even if you were a miracle of modern science, I think 137 is a bit more than you can count on.

Now it's not **necessarily** morbid to think about such things. It can actually be quite freeing. Incredibly freeing. Once you know about how much time you have, then you know just about how much money you need. Which means that after you make the proper provisions for emergencies, long-term medical care, and gifting (as we shall call "inheritance"), all the rest is gravy. Honest.

Your Retirement Income

In the distant past (BI = Before Internet), the standard approach advised for retirement planning was to save until you could live off the interest of your savings. Furthermore, this savings was to be held in "secure" investments such as CD's or government bonds, which generally would generate a return of about 8%. This means that in order to receive an annual income of $80,000, you would have needed to sock away $1,000,000, which then would have had to stay there, untouched. This way, if you lived forever, you would have had an income of

$80,000 a year on which to do it. And if you didn't manage immortality, and did fall off your perch, you would be leaving $1,000,000 behind.[1]

In today's economy, a mix of investments at various tiers of risk would probably be a better choice for the investment approach. Taking that same $1,000,000 and splitting it into three parts:

$400,000	in CDs	at 8%
$400,000	in Mutual Funds	at 15%
$200,000	in Stocks	at 15%

would give you an annual income of $122,000, or.[2]

$32,000 from CDs
$60,000 from Mutual Funds
$30,000 from Stocks.

This does sound a bit better than the previous model (a 43% increase), but it still means that you will have a constant income - forever. Or rather, that you will leave $1,000,000 on the perch behind you when you fall off.

Why was that $1,000,000 left behind? What was the purpose of it to begin with? It was to provide you with an income into the year 2080? Of course not. Was it to leave a burden for your children to acquire at your passing? Even if that thought did cross your mind, is that actually necessary or healthy for them. It means your sitting around doing nothing for thirty years, or the only way to go about financially enriching their lives? No. No, it isn't. So what was the point of holding onto all that money until the very end? It was simply a means of providing you and your family with a happy and secure life in your latter years. It was an attempt to ensure life, not one to insure death.

So you had the right idea. That money was to be used for life. But life is being lived right now! And the life you want to lead, can lead, will

---

[1] These financial figures are merely basic examples.
[2] Your particular income may also include pensions, Social Security, and/or rental income. All the better since you do not need to rely on "savings" alone.

lead is your newly chosen life, the walking of your new Chen-Tao in these post-Kaneka years. The question then is - how do you reconcile the desire to start out on your Chen-Tao with your sense of uncertainty and insecurity about what the future might bring, and with your concerns for the needs of your children and grandchildren?

These four simple steps you can take that will enable you to feel comfortable pushing your (actively) retired financial gondola back into the stream of life. These steps, once accomplished, will enable you to look at your future income in a whole new light.

1. Develop a financial plan to cover medical care and emergencies.
2. Determine a method of covering the financial burden of long-term care.
3. Determine the amount of money you want to gift to your children, grandchildren, relatives, or charities.
4. Determine the amount you want them to inherit when you finally do fall off the perch.

Once you've developed these plans and thereby put your mind at rest, you will find you are able to proceed confidently down your Chen-Tao!

1. Medical Care: Buy the very best health insurance available.

It is common sense, really. Prior to being eligible for Medicare, be sure you have the best insurance plan you can find. Post Medicare, choose the best supplemental medical provider. Carefully study all the policies so you are aware of what they do and do not cover, and what the requirements are for maintaining coverage of all allowed procedures. Place additional money aside for medical procedures that might not be covered, or identify additional sources of income that can be earmarked for such a purpose (we will talk about various sources later). Now your medical care is fully covered. There is no more need to worry. Honest.

As far as choosing medical coverage, there are three types of health insurance: HMO, PPO, and fee-for-service. HMOs cost the least because they give you the least control over your medical care. Forget about HMO's. I haven't heard of a good one yet. HMOs are for young people with perfect health, or young families who can't afford more yet. You are neither of these. The best type of insurance for you is fee-for-service, and it is the best for the exact same reason that HMOs are the worst. In fee-for-service you are the one in control of your medical care. You can choose any physician you please and generally you can see any specialist you care to without needing prior primary physician approval.

If you don't have Medicare, this is obviously going to be the most expensive insurance option, but there are ways to keep the costs down. Given that you are in a position to have access to emergency cash, one of the best ways to cut costs is to raise the deductible. In the case of one Wenjen who had a preexisting condition before she switched her insurance policy, she was able to cut her new premium in half, simply by raising the annual deductible from $1,500 to $5,000. Even if she were to need to spend the $5,000, it would still be less than the amount she would have spent on the higher premium. Assuming she stays healthy, wealthy, and wise, this is $5,000 she gets to put back into traveling her Chen-Tao every year!

Another option is to find out if your doctor is in a PPO. PPOs manage to be less expensive than fee-for-service by allowing you to control your own medical care - within a pre-prescribed group of physicians. Often they will allow you to see doctors outside the group but cover only a percentage of the total cost. You will need to consult the plan to see what each individual PPO offers. Read it carefully. Your life may depend on it.

2. Long-Term Care: Something we don't like to talk about, but which will probably enter your life path at some point.

Long-term care is what makes most of us crazy when it comes to trying to plan for our future. Many advisors recommend long-term care insurance. Personally, I dislike most forms of insurance, and this one is close to the top of my list. It is expensive, full of exclusions, and generally a tricky proposition. If you really feel you want to have it, make sure your attorney reads all the fine print.

My best advice when considering of long-term care would be to free your mind. Remember, you are affluent; therefore you have many alternatives. Currently the cost of a good nursing home is between $40,000 and $60,000 a year. Based on the previous $1,000,000 example, you easily could afford your care and still ensure a decent quality of life for your partner. If both of you needed long-term care simultaneously, you could still manage it and find your costs potentially decreasing. But there are other, more creative ways of financing your long-term and emergency medical care, and we will discuss them after we take care of one more step.

3. Gifting: Children, Grandchildren, Gifts & Inheritance

I believe in supporting and caring for one's children at every stage of their life path. This Wenjen attitude toward support and caring is different from that of many other people. Wenjens are unique and enlightened individuals who understand the value and finite breadth of life and therefore are dedicated to living life fully, right here, right now. You are a Wenjen. Your attitude extends not just to your life, but also to the lives of those you love. For this reason, I encourage you to enrich the lives of your children (and grandchildren) *as they are living it now*. What is the point of helping them only after you are no longer around? You have more to give them than just money anyway. Most important, you give them love. And you can give money in more loving ways than others. If you want to enrich their lives, and at the same time have your own life enriched, change your concept of simply leaving an inheritance to your children in death, to one of gifting to your children while you are still alive. You will find that taking this step not only allows you freedom, but allows your children to feel your love as coming directly from you, rather than through a mere piece of paper called a will.

These are my three rules for giving money to one's family:

Rule 1: Give while you are alive!

A gift of $10,000[3] at age 21 for a car, or $20,000 at age 25 for a down payment on a house, will probably be much more appreciated than $50,000 at age 50. And you will be here to see the gifts enjoyed. You may even have the pleasure of getting a genuine thank you from your son or daughter (maybe even a hug) in this world instead of the next.

---

[3] You can give up to $10,000 as a gift without having to file a tax return. Your partner can gift the same amount.

Rule 2: Establish a trust fund to give a financial boost at crucial times in their lives.

This could be a graduate degree, a down payment on a house, the medical bills for a new grandchild, or the starting of a business. The cost of education is rising by the minute. Setting up an educational trust for grandchildren may be the best help you can give to launch them into the adult world.

Here are things that some of the Wenjens I have interviewed have done:

- A Gift of $10,000 at 20 years for a car.
- A Gift of $20,000 a year at 22 years to complete an MBA.
- A Gift of $20,000 at 26 years, a down payment on a house.
- A Gift of $20,000 plus a loan of $20,000 to start a business.

Rule 3: OK, so give them a little extra, too.

In my opinion, it is not beneficial for children (adults) to inherit too much money. In some cases it can flat out kill initiative. If a twenty-something is getting an income of $10,000 a month from a trust fund, he or she might not be very inclined to take a challenging yet career-starting job at only $3,000 a month. In other cases, an inheritance can push children down a life path that maybe is not theirs. Perhaps creating a country-club lifestyle for them that maybe inappropriate for their age or experience. And perhaps worst of all, the handing over of a large amount of money to your child at too young of an age can deprive them the life experiences that are needed to learn how to manage, invest, and create further income for themselves and for their own family well into the future, and long after you are gone.

In contrast, a healthy inheritance later in life can give your children a jump on their own retirement financial planning. However, assuming you have enabled them to become active, healthy individuals all along the way, they should already have a fairly good start. Yes, leave them some money; but no, it doesn't have to be all of your money. Decide what you want to give them for their latter years, and balance that with what you want to give yourself for *your* latter years. After all, I am sure your children love you and want to see you enjoy your latter years as much as you want to provide for theirs. Somewhere there is a number that is lovingly respectful of both their eventual Kanekas and your current one.

The following is a sample worksheet to help give you an idea of how to structure a gifting and Active-Retirement financial plan:

Age	Amount	Purpose
Daughter - Janice Smith (& Husband)		
28	$20,000	Home
30	$20,000	Business Start-Up
31	$20,000	Business Re-Investment
--	$250,000	Inheritance
Son - Pete Smith (& Family: Cindy, Pete Jr., kids)		
30	$10,000	Addition to Home
42	$10,000	College for Cindy
43	$20,000	College for Cindy & Pete, Jr.
44	$20,000	College for Cindy & Pete, Jr.
45	$10,000	College for Pete, Jr.
46	$10,000	College for Pete, Jr.
--	$250,000	Inheritance

Age	Amount	Purpose
Granddaughter - Cindy Smith		
17	$10,000	Car
22	$20,000	Grad School

28	$20,000	House
--	$150,000	Inheritance
Grandson - Pete Smith, Jr.		
17	$10,000	Car
25	$20,000	Business Start-Up
28	$20,000	House
--	$150,000	Inheritance

You get the picture. Now create a similar chart for yourself in your Kaneka Journal. Use as much space as you need. This should be looked at as a working document that should be reviewed annually. An estate planner to find the best way to fund the trusts and inheritance should also review it.

But where does it come from?

So now you have a solid plan for providing for your health care, your and your partner's long-term care, and your children and grandchildren's well-being. But these things do cost money. And if you add these costs to your general expenses, and then to the costs of your new Big List items, you may begin to wonder where all the money is supposed to come from.

Well, now that you are no longer so concerned about hoarding all your assets for posterity or in case disaster strikes, there are plenty of alternative sources of income to fund everything you want and need to do.

Some immediate alternatives are:[4]

- Equity Loan (2nd mortgage)
- Reverse Mortgage (they pay you!)

---

[4] A good book on the general subject of utilizing your assets in this life is Stephen Pollan's *Die Broke*.

- Refinancing Your House
- Refinancing Other Real Estate

And finally, the great heresy of retirement financial planning...

- Using part of your principal
  (It's your money, after all)

[1]There are many alternatives, and ultimately you should find a competent and imaginative financial planner who can help you design a plan that will work best for you with your actual assets.

Before you slam this book shut, I want to reemphasize that during a Kaneka, there are no sacred cows. And that includes principal. I am not suggesting that you run out and spend $1,000,000 on a yacht for that Caribbean adventure, if you only have $1,000,000 in principal. But I am suggesting that you consider the possibility of spending, say, 3% or 5% of your stock principal a year. And why not? Your health, long-term care, and children are all being taken care of; you certainly will have enough remaining to handle your annual expenses (at least $20,000 more a year than if you had invested the old way - even without any of your stock dividends); and you have finally realized that you have a responsibility to actually *live* the rest of your life. And you can!

A Wenjen never says, "I cannot do this because I cannot afford it." All right, in the long run that might be true (and so you rent a yacht instead), but you need to get beyond the fear that you cannot spend your money because you might run out of it. Get comfortable with your money. You are not going to run out of it because you have already provided for every emergency. And you are not going to stay on that perch forever - so what is wrong with taking the equity out of your home now? You are not being "selfish" - you have already provided for your children and their future - in this life! They will be as secure as you could ever make them even after you pass on, which leaves no more reason for you to hoard money to provide for anyone until the year 2080. You can begin to spend your money now, on dreams you have now. You can live your life in this very special period of time - your time as an honorable Wenjen.

Summing Up

There is no reason to panic about financing your Active-Retirement once you accept that you have a finite amount of time before you fall off the perch. As a result, if you open your mind and allow your financial outlook to undergo a Kaneka as well, you will find that there is more than enough money for both your Big List items and to take care of your and your family's well-being. Here are a few simple steps you can take to ensure this:

1. Identify your Active-Retirement income and update your investment strategy (if necessary) to allow you the greatest gains.
2. Develop a financial plan to cover medical care and emergencies.
3. Determine a method of covering the financial burden of long-term care.
4. Determine the amount of money you want to gift to your children, grandchildren, charities, etc.
5. Determine the amount you want them to inherit when you finally do fall off the perch.
6. Now that everyone and everyone's future is taken care of, come up with a plan to **utilize** your assets - in this life. Immediate suggestions are equity loans, reverse mortgages, refinancing of home or other real estate, or even spending a small percentage of your principal each year.
7. Find an **imaginative** financial advisor who can lead you to the alternatives that are best for your individual situation.

Lifestyles of the Affluent and Obscure
Where you live and why you live there

If you always do what you always did,
you'll always get what you always got.
~ Unknown ~

Do I Want to Go On Living as I Always Have?

We have discussed the "mental attitude" of the Kaneka.[1] It is a "can do," "want to do" and "will do" attitude. An attitude that begins to develop as soon as you choose the activities you really want to pursue. For you, it began when you created your Big List. You can actually prove to yourself that this metamorphosis has already begun simply by reading over your list again. Upon re-visiting your fondest hopes, dreams, and repeated pleasures, you will feel the excitement and expectation just welling up within you. And why not? This is a list of your favorite things. Just reading over it can make you want to run out and grab the world. Knowing what you want can be that inspirational.

Still, your Big List is very "future" oriented. It is all about what you want to do – in the future. It says very little about what you are doing in the present. So how do you connect the two? We know that the present is the place where every future begins. That is why I use the metaphor of a path. Because of your Kaneka, this journey will be a particularly dynamic and fulfilling one. However, if there seems to be a big discrepancy between your current lifestyle and the future activities you desire, a road needs to be cleared between the two. To clear a path toward your desired future, you will need to examine and understand your current lifestyle and what might be clogging it.

A significant number of people I interviewed never seemed willing to examine their lifestyles as a part of the decision-making process required for Kaneka. But for your Kaneka, I am going to ask you many times in the course of this book to examine yourself and your life. So I want to stress again that considering options does not mean that anything is going to change. It just means that you are giving yourself the opportunity to come up with something that you might *like* to change. This book is all about finding the lifestyle that *you* want. This is not about my or anyone else (even your faithful, well-meaning partner) telling you how you should best spend your time. It is about you discovering what you want to do, how to do it, and then getting it done.

---

[1] Kaneka: a rebirth into Active-Retirement

So, I will try my best not to let my prejudices come into play, if you promise to do the same.

So let's begin by looking at the basic elements that make up your present: Time, Space and Being. Time is something that you suddenly have a lot more of. Space is where you exist. And Being is all that exists (which if you've looked in your attic recently, is quite a lot!).

These are the elements of your present that you will have to accept, change, or organize to reach your desired future. Fortunately, you have already begun to address Time. When you created your Big List, you decided how you wanted to spend your time in the future, and you even went so far as to schedule events. But that alone will not ensure that your future lifestyle will be appropriate for your eventual Wenjen[2] self. There is still Space and Being to contend with. They don't just go away (or get out of the way) because you've scheduled things you would like to do. So let us take a macro look at Space and Being.

Changing on the Macro Level

For most of us, the things we have are kept in our house, apartment, or condo. And for most of us, the biggest thing we own is our house. Even if you only rent, your home (and the stuff in it) is still the center of your life anchoring you to a certain place and in many ways a certain lifestyle. So we will begin our examination of your current lifestyle with your home/house/castle, because it is the root of your present lifestyle – especially now that work isn't there to put its two cents in.

The hardest and most important decision in your Kaneka is determining what place your current home will have in your future life. You probably have lived in your current home for many years, your children might have grown up there, you know each plant, the garage and/or the attic is full of mementos and you've finally paid off your mortgage. And now you may be thinking, "This guy, whose book I spent good money on, is going to tell me to get rid of my home?!?"

No, that is not really what I am going to do. I simply believe you should *examine* your emotional attachment to your house and look at its financial and lifestyle implications. After doing that, you may still

---

[2] Wenjen: the affluent person who is enlightened enough to spend his or her time pursuing a "cultured" life.

conclude that you want to keep your house, though you may decide to remodel it to adapt it to your Wenjen lifestyle. Or you may realize you want to sell your house, buy a condo in the city, and extend your lifestyle to other locations. Or you may want to move to other locations altogether. Regardless of what you choose, if you have taken the opportunity to examine what type of home will best serve you as you travel your Chen-Tao,[3] you can be sure that this home will nurture the Wenjen lifestyle you have chosen for your future. Without taking this step, your Kaneka cannot be complete.

So first, identify what you get and what you really want from your "home." Be realistic — if you had to buy a new home tomorrow, taking your current situation into account, would you really buy a four-bedroom house in the suburb of a smog-laden city?

Again, I can hear the protests. "I have lived here for the last thirty years. I know the neighborhood (that wonderful Ralphs, the best Starbucks, the Gap, my dry cleaners that only charges a dollar a shirt but still gets it right – and I'll never find another shoe-repair man like Frank!). I know all the neighbors (even though I don't get along with many of them). All my friends live in this city (although we seem to be too busy to see them often). We have season tickets to the theatre. And the list goes on and on.

Open your mind. You may come back to exactly where you started, but the journey around your lifestyle may still give you some insight into how to create your desired future.

Let's do a basic list of pros and cons of your present home. A list could look something like this:

PROS

1. I've made a wonderful garden that I enjoy spending time in and love working on.
2. The kitchen has everything I need and I know what is in every cupboard.
3. My children grew up here and it feels like home.
4. Most of my friends live in this town.

---

[3] ChenTao: The right life path for you.

CONS

1. It's a big house and a lot to clean and keep up.
2. There is heavy traffic on the street.
3. My children and grandchildren live five hundred miles away.
4. If we are going to stay here, we really should put a significant amount of money into the house to make it properly fit our new lifestyle.

Now make your own list of pros and cons. As there is no way to judge how long this list might become — write it in your Kaneka Journal. If you have a partner, create this list together. Joint investments require joint consideration.

Give yourself five minutes to list "pros" and five more to list "cons."

Once you have identified the pros and cons, the next set of questions just leaps out. Examine your answers, looking for any drawbacks or benefits to each one. Going back to my example, one might create a list like this:

PRO... but,

1. Would I be willing to start my garden over, perhaps smaller, and someplace else? Would I enjoy it more if it were easier to maintain?
2. Do I really need all those gadgets in the kitchen to cook what I'm eating now? Do I really need the electric pepper mill or the pneumatic wine opener?
3. Would our house feel more like home if we were able to see our children and their families more regularly?
4. How often do I really see my friends and how much time do I spend with them?

CONS... but,

1. I could hire someone to do the cleaning. Or get a tenant who could care for the house when we are away.
2. I've dealt with the traffic for years. It won't kill me to do it some more.

3. How much time do I want to spend with my children (and do they really want to see me that much) and what kind of activities would I really like us to share?

4. Fixing up the house would be a worthwhile expense. It would make this a better home to live in for the next thirty years.

Go ahead and do your own "pros...but" and "cons...but" lists. Give yourself ten minutes for each.

Some ideas probably came to mind immediately from these "but" lists: "Another thirty years?! I don't think I want to live in the city another thirty years!" "Are my son and his wife really going to live in Boston forever, or are they going to just move again in the next few years? Maybe I need to consider a way we can vacation or travel together as a family." This is good. The electrons are beginning to flow. You are beginning to see that a different choice in housing could add benefits to your life.

What alternative housing options do you have?

• A condo on the beach?

• A house in the mountains where family can ski in the winter and swim in the summer?

• A house in the country that is close enough to the city that you can comfortably commute into the city once or twice a week?

• An apartment in the city and buying (or leasing) a second home out of town?

• A condo in the city and renting homes (or apartments) abroad for weeks or months at a time?

• A houseboat and a house in the mountains?

Now fill in your own ideas;

- _____

  _____ ?

- _____

  _____ ?

- _____

  _____ ?

What would it be like to choose one of these options instead of holding on to your current home? Would a condo in the city cost you less, make it easier to travel, and still let you see your friends and keep your season tickets to the theatre (not to mention your favorite Safeway, Starbucks and Gap)? If you allow yourself to consider any living situation that comes to mind, more and more options for your future lifestyle will appear.

So put your (and your partner's) Big List on the table and pretend you have chosen an alternative housing option. Consider what your life would be like as you pursued your Big List goals. Let your mind go. Then consider another housing option in light of your Big List. And another. Do not censor any idea. You can reject choices later, but now take your morning coffee and sit with your Kaneka Journal and explore all your housing options and the repercussions they could have in your future life.

Give yourself twenty minutes.

Excellent!   This concept of changing homes, or having multiple homes or long-term rentals may indeed be very new to you. It is designed to liberate you from your past. Already, I can hear the trees of resistance falling and the brambles of inflexibility being cut back as a road to your future begins to be cleared. Now that you are at least open to the idea of a different housing situation, there are a few things to keep in mind:

Location

Consider what is important to you. Is it the weather, or the opera, attending a football game or being able to sail most of the year. Every time my wife and I lease a place in another location and it rains, snows, or engulfs us in a tornado, my wife reminds me that the weather back home in Los Angeles is a sunny 78 degrees.

Location is very important. Every year a number of magazines publish lists of the "best" places to live, but what is good for you now as a Wenjen, might not have been good for you when you and your partner were starting out with two young children oh so many years ago. Location should be chosen (or re-chosen) based on your desires now; that is, based on the Big List. But keep in mind your day-to-day quality of life. Some people are partial to a good public transportation system (Chicago has a fantastic one). Personally, I like warm, sunny weather (Los Angeles is more my speed). It's all about priorities.

Here are the priorities of some of the people I interviewed:

Relationships: Being near family and friends. This is very important, but shouldn't be the only factor.

Culture: The symphony, plays, museums, lectures, foreign films or whatever you define as culture.

Weather: No extremes. (One out of three people who retire to Florida leave because of the hot humid summers. And don't even consider visiting Chicago in January, regardless of the heaters at all of the elevated train stops.)

Good healthcare: Some people like it. All hospitals are not created equal.

Educational opportunities: Adult education, access to college libraries and courses, access to hobby or sport- specific classes.

Nearby sporting events: Having a good baseball, football or basketballs team in your town. It allows you to attend live sporting events.

People with similar views: You need to have people around who you can relate to. People who share a common background in education, politics, religion, or lifestyle. Commonality is important for me. I loved Santa Cruz, but it was a little too "60's" for me and though Phoenix was nicely sunny, it ran a little too Republican for my tastes.

Things Important in a Location   Rank

- _____   _____

- _____   _____

- _____   _____

- _____   _____

- _____   _____

- _____   _____

- _____   _____

Low crime rate: Security is important. You want to enjoy your life without fear. And you want to be able to leave your home with peace of mind. No place is completely free of crime but some areas are much better than others.

Taxes: Some people consider taxes to be an important factor in where they choose to live. There are a number of different taxes that may affect you: income tax, sales tax, and estate tax. Personally, I don't believe this should be a major consideration in choosing where to live. If you have a good CPA and tax advisor, you should be able to handle potential tax problems in other ways. Finally, if you find that you can't avoid the tax issues a particular area might bring -- well, it's no crime to pay taxes and you can afford to.

The above eight criteria are not listed in any specific order. Different ones may be more important to you than others. Some of them might be specific to your Big List. If golf is your god, then living near the best golf courses may be the most important criteria. If you suffer from hay fever, well, then I don't have to tell you...

Make a list of eight things you feel you need to have in a city, town, or area. When you are done, go back and rank them in importance.

A Second Home

At various times in your life you probably dreamed of having a second home. Possibly a vacation home in the mountains or on the beach. When my wife and I had three small children, a dog, and a maid, I found that owning a condo at Mammoth Mountain was wonderful. With our more than one hundred ski-related items stored at the condo, skiing was suddenly as easy as a morning's drive, and as a result we skied more often. But as the kids got older, they decided they wanted to ski other places – sometimes with us (if we paid), and sometimes on their own (we still paid), and so the condo no longer remained necessary or even cost effective, and we sold it. With no Mammoth condo to limit us we found that it had removed the psychological impetus to go to Mammoth. We expanded our horizons to skiing in Aspen, Vail, Park City, and even Europe.

Although owning a vacation home makes it easy to get away it tends to obligate you to use it and return repeatedly to the same spot. This may not fit into a lifestyle designed to achieve your heart's desires.

The Permanent Vacation

Some people decide to move to a place they have really enjoyed on their vacations. This is usually a mistake. The place you loved for one or two weeks can become very boring after twenty or thirty. But if you are seriously considering it, first rent a condo or house in the area for a month. Try to rent in the style and level in which you think you might want to live. Don't rent a house right on the beach if that's not what you are going to buy. This will give you a taste of what living in there might be like. Before signing anything also make sure to visit the area in the off-season, when you have to either shovel the snow every morning or stay inside with the air-conditioning.

Renting Apartments, Condos, or Houses

In contrast to owning, I have always preferred renting a second home at a mountain, beach, ski, or other vacation area. You can also stay in a hotel if you are really attached to maid service, but a house or condo will offer you a kitchen, living room, and probably a couple of bedrooms so that friends and children can visit. Currently, we have a house in the city where we have lived for many years, and we lease apartments or houses in several places for two weeks to a month throughout the year.

There are a number of ways to rent houses. When I decided that I wanted to spend part of the summer in Carmel, I subscribed to the Sunday edition of its weekly paper. In the classifieds I found property management companies that offered homes for rent on a monthly basis. I contacted a few of these agencies and gave them my requirements. They sent me pictures and prices. After we had narrowed it down to two specific houses, I asked my wife if she would call the agencies and ask detailed questions like street proximity, house condition, and furnishings. She did such a wonderful job that when we arrived at the chosen house, I was about ready to buy it.

Other methods of obtaining information include, as always, the Internet. We also belong to an organization called "Hideaways"[4] that lists houses and apartments all over the world that are available for short periods of time. There are also always ads in the Sunday edition of *The New York Times* and in sports or activities magazines like *Ski*, *Outside*, and *Golf*.

Housing Exchanges

You can easily find housing exchanges of all kinds over the Internet. The idea behind an exchange is that you allow someone (or a family) from overseas to stay in your home while you stay overseas in theirs. Often this includes having access to their vehicles, maid service, and other amenities. I recommend www.homeexchange.com which can connect you to high-scale homes for exchange, from Ireland to Africa to Maine. In most cases pictures of the interiors or views from the homes are included. There are many lovely homes and apartments available for exchange, from a simple (but elegant) wood cabin on the beach in Australia to a designer houseboat on the Seine to an entire estate in South Africa. Some come with acres of land to explore and others offer addresses along some of the most desired avenues in the world. The Web site also has an easy search program that allows you to quickly find

---

[4] Hideaways can be found online at www.hideaways.com or you can contact them at Hideaways International, Inc., 767 Islington St., Portsmouth, NH 03801 (603) 430-4433 or toll-free (877) 843-4433.

either people in your desired location who are offering their homes or people who are wanting to travel to your neck of the woods.

However, I would like to caution you before you leap into a home exchange situation. For those of you who have irreplaceable pieces of art or items of sentimental value in your home, you might want to think twice before doing a housing exchange. Housing exchanges may give you the opportunity to live overseas at the level to which you have become accustomed, but they also allow someone you don't know to do the same in your place (and perhaps with your vehicles). Different people (especially of different cultures) often have very different ideas of how to live, which is one of the wonderful things about traveling abroad. But carefully consider the situation before you allow someone to come and live among your most precious objects without you being there to supervise. I mention it only because my wife and I know of a few people who have had unfortunate experiences. A home exchange may not be wise for everyone. Being affluent you have the means to rent anyplace you like. Nonetheless, if the idea still appeals to you, take the time to get to know your candidates (why not make it an opportunity for a little visit?) and make sure to get several strong recommendations before committing to anyone.

Moving Abroad

Living permanently abroad has some advantages over living in the United States and in many cases can be done cheaper. However, it requires careful evaluation. It may sound great to have a castle in Britain (with no insulation) or a house in Southern France (with no phone), but if you are used to the services and facilities you have here, you might find actual life abroad rather burdensome. Again, my advice would be to rent an apartment for a month and see how you enjoy actual life in the area. It will probably be a revelation to you. Language is only a one of the problems you may encounter. People you thought quaint could appear quite different in the contact your day-to-day situations. The fact that in Italy it can take months before phone service is installed could make it hard to stay in touch with friends and family. If you enjoy films, it can be frustrating to see Mel Gibson chattering away (dubbed) in a language you don't yet fully understand. The lack of access to books in your language could be a major setback to your long-term mental health (though as long as you actually do have phone service there is, Amazon.com).

My intention is not to discourage anyone from any idea. Many interesting things can happen when you live abroad. Ultimately, you are the only one who can decide what is best for you. My only advice is to take it slowly enough that you reach an **informed** decision.

Changing on the Micro Level

As you redesign the space you live in, the stuff you put into it needs to change as well. But this again is an opportunity to bring your present more closely in line with the future you desire.

Cars

Unless cars are your passion, they are very much a product of your location, your needs, or your lifestyle. You do not want an SUV if you are planning to move to Oxford, England (or Manhattan for that matter). You do not want your only car to be a Karman Ghia if you are moving to Aspen. You also need to consider your needs. Do you pick up plants or lumber at Home Depot. Do you take your bicycles surfboard and skis with you everywhere you go? Or perhaps you like to buy large birdcages at swap meets? In any of these cases a SUV can be very useful. However you should consider that things you hold onto from the past may become an obstacle to your new life. Instead, choosing the right tool for the job (even if that job is just to have fun) is the way to look at the objects in a Wenjen's life.

Clothes

Clothes should be responsive to both your personal taste and your needs for the Big List. Do you need (want) more formal clothes as you begin to attend the opera more regularly? Or would four more pairs of jeans really be a fitting purchase for the man or woman who plans to sit at the lake house and finally write that novel?

Furniture, Books, Trinkets, et al.

Some, really a few, people can clean out their own homes and give or throw things away. In many cases they will just pick up an object and decide to reminisce or put off the decision to give it away. "Someday maybe the kids will want it, or "this is almost and antique" are two great lines developed by people as the clean up their house. A new one only recently developed, "I'll wait and take it to the Antique Road show." If you are a packrat of a procrastinator I suggest you hire an organizer to work with you and help you organize and get rid of anything superfluous in your house. Whether you are committed to moving into a smaller condo so that you can gallivant about the globe or staying in your home and building a kiln in your backyard it is important to have someone come in and weed through the objects -- eliminating the unnecessary ones and bringing the needed ones into a non-chaotic state so that you can spend your time and energy on something more important -- like enjoying your life!

Summing Up

Now that you have made your Big List plans, it is time to look at your day-to-day life and reshape it to suit your new path. The biggest step in that transformation is evaluating and understanding the role your current home will play in your future.   To that end I suggest the following exercises.

1. List the pros and cons of your current housing situation.
2. Review these lists and make lists of "pros...but" and "cons...but" to look at both sides of the issues.
3. List any alternative housing situation that comes to mind (especially if it appeals to you!).
4. Writing in your Kaneka Journal, pretend you have chosen one of these alternative situations. Then review your Big List items. Write out what your future life would be like in this new situation. Do this with as many different housing alternatives as you can in twenty minutes.
5. Make a list of eight factors that are important to you in choosing a location. Order them by rank.
6. Consider various types of housing arrangements --exchanges, moving abroad, buying a second home or short-term renting and determine how any of them would improve your future lifestyle.
7. Once you have chosen the appropriate housing situation for your Wenjen lifestyle, commit to revamping your possessions on the

micro level.   Review them with your Big List goals in mind. The either get rid of the unnecessary things yourself or hire an organizer to help you make it all work.

Anyone who stops learning is old, whether at twenty or eighty.
Anyone who keeps learning stays young. The greatest thing in
life is to keep your mind young.
~ Henry Ford ~

The growth of the human mind is still high adventure, in many
ways the highest adventure on earth.
~ Norman Cousins ~

When you were active in the workplace there were always intellectual and creative challenges. Beyond the performance of your job, you had to stay on top of the constant changes in your field. To do that you had to read journals, trade magazines, and books. You discussed new methods, technologies, or ideas with coworkers and attended seminars or classes. You were constantly learning, just by the nature of being an active member of your vocation.

Now that you are pursuing new goals, you still need access to information. You need to read journals, books, and take classes. You are not going to an office every day where tasks are laid out for you. Instead, you must make the opportunity yourself.

Depending on the extent you want to immerse yourself in your chosen pursuit, this could be quite an easy task. Becoming a full-time student or taking an immersion course in your chosen area could put you in an environment totally geared toward that goal. Or, if you want the freedom to pursue things at your own pace or in a time frame that is more flexible to your (or your partner's) Kaneka plans, then there are other options that can work just as well. The key is, as always, to find the way that works best for you, and implement it!

Classes Big and Small

Many people like the in-depth instruction by experts and the enjoyment of a group of peers that taking classes can offer. However, classes can mean anything from going for a Ph.D. in Religious Studies at Harvard to taking classical guitar at the local music shop. Find whatever type of class meets your goals. First, you need to decide how seriously you want to pursue the chosen activity. For example, will a watercolor course at Anne's Art Activities give you the basic skills you need to paint, or do you need to study painting at The Art Institute of Chicago? You are the only one who knows what you want to accomplish. Have the courage to admit to *exactly* what it is – and then go out and find the class or program that will teach you everything you need!

Starting Small

University Extension and Community and City Colleges Adult education is a serious business. The UCLA extension catalog runs to 240 pages. It has classes ranging from "The Magnetic Focus of a Dwarf Star" to "Choosing a Dog to Fit Your Personality", as well as classes specifically designed for seniors. City and community colleges usually offer adult education courses. Generally, classes meet one or two nights a week, for eight to sixteen weeks, and are offered at different levels to meet students' levels of expertise. This can be a great way to fit education into your other plans, or to acquire education on numerous topics if you have a particularly rangy mind. Personally, I have a hard time sitting still for three hours, especially from 7:00 to 10:00 PM. I attribute some of that impatience to the influence of the television remote. Not only has it gotten my average viewing time for a single program down to only 52 seconds but I'm now used to watching at least three shows at a time.

Seminars and Workshops: If weeks of evening classes don't appeal to you, there are weekend programs and workshops available. Topics range from autobiographical writing to auto repair and from stock market investing to sculpting. Seminars and workshops are often listed in the same catalogs as university or college extension programs, but many places that host these seminars publish separate adult education bulletins as well. Parks and Recreation centers, coffee shops, and bookstores will generally carry these bulletins and have bulletin boards on which additional workshops are posted. Local papers will often list upcoming events. Retail stores also hold workshops in a particular field. For example, CompUSA offers classes on computers, ranging from the very fundamentals to networking servers, and Home Depot offers classes in house repair.

Classes: If you need more flexibility in your schedule there are other schools that might meet your needs. Local schools for art, music, computers, language, and other activities are quite common. Classes are usually offered in both group and private lessons, with private lessons providing the most flexibility. Group classes usually are offered in short segments or on an ongoing basis. Both enable you to travel while still progressing in your skills by allowing you to take classes whenever you are in town. Classes taken on an ongoing basis allow you the further flexibility of picking a class any time you find it convenient. Clearly the best part of schools such as these is that most schedule the majority of their classes on the weekends or during the day when some of us feel most attentive!

Societies, Groups, and Clubs: Joining a society, group, or club can offer you a lot of the advantages of taking a class, while allowing you access to activities as well. By joining a political, environmental, or other activist group you can gain access to a group of intelligent peers, a network of journals and newsletters, a series of lectures and workshops in the field, and the ability to participate in numerous activities based on an idea that you believe in. Groups like the Sierra Club offer opportunities for intelligent environmental and political activism and for taking scheduled hikes with other club members.

Book clubs are another interesting way to expand your horizons. Most book clubs meet once a month. If you attend one and find you don't like the club or its particular choices, it is easy to change clubs or simply form your own. Creating your own book club is a very good way of reading all the books you said you wanted to read when you retired.

Activity groups are another way of finding companionship while accomplishing Kaneka plans. There are groups that tour museums, galleries, or places of architectural or historic interest. Attending or creating a writing group for poetry, novels, or journal writing can offer the support and encouragement that can make completing goals seem easy. There is no reason that a group for any artistic or intellectual activity cannot be created and the benefit of companionship (and commitment!) thereby gained.

Existing clubs, societies, and groups often advertise their meetings in the community listing sections of local newspapers. Churches, specialty stores (like bookstores or hiking stores), art centers, recreation centers, and the Internet are other good resources of finding when and where groups are meeting. Even the Yellow Pages list some of the more established groups. With a little research you should easily be able to find (or create) the group or club that fits your goals – from there it is simply a matter of signing up and getting started! (You can join alone or with your partner, though if you are no longer "going to the office" and are already spending a lot of time with your partner, you may find a new group to be a welcome solo enterprise.)

Classes Offered over the Internet: There is a growing field of experts offering on-line programs. You can learn journalistic writing, study poetry, or earn a degree. The clear advantage to these types of classes is that you never need to even leave your home (or your computer, if it is traveling with you). Internet classes also allow you maximum flexibility – you can do the work and "attend" the class whenever you squeeze it in. The only process you will miss out on is the creation of a peer group, though a small number of classes do allow student-to-student participation and critique. In some ways, Internet classes are the cutting edge in tailor-made education. Just make sure that with all this ease you don't forget that most on-line classes function like regular classes – with all the requirements and deadlines that generally apply.

And Getting Bigger

Immersion Courses: Immersion courses are most often identified with language, but there are immersion courses for art history, computers, photography, painting, filmmaking, music, and much more. These classes offer you the level of quality and specificity of a university program with a much smaller outlay of time. Although they can be quite intense, if you are more interested in practicing your Spanish on actual Spaniards than in spending your time in school they might be just what you're looking for. These courses will allow you to get a working mastery of your topic in four, six, or twelve weeks.

IMMERSION COURSES

So, if painting in Spain was really what you had in mind, you can get both the Spanish and the painting techniques down by next spring – just in time for the running of the bulls!

Study Abroad: Many schools and universities offer study abroad programs that can range in length from a few weeks to a year. I am thinking of programs that are geared toward foreigners (you), are generally taught in one's own language (unless you are taking language courses), and that typically include opportunities for side trips in and around the area. What better way to study Mozart than in Vienna? How about studying art of the Renaissance in Florence or Shakespeare at Oxford? This type of study offers you the opportunity to combine two or more of your Kaneka plans. For example, if you are planning on going to the Salzburg Music Festival, wouldn't taking a music appreciation course there first really heighten the experience?

Entering a foreign university as a regular student is a very valid option – just make sure you take a good language intensive first if you want to keep up!

Colleges: "Going back to school" obviously offers one of the most intense learning experiences of all. Every activity required of you is directed toward your learning. However, even if you attend them part-time, most programs require a healthy commitment of your time. And although it might seem like a joy to be able to sit and read all day, day after day – do not forget – you will be tested and asked to write papers! If this sounds exactly like your cup of tea, there is no reason you should not go back for that second (or first) bachelor's in an entirely different area than you studied before. Just make sure they waive any required courses you might already have taken previously. Who wants to wade through geometry again if you are trying to study European History? If you find your new college won't waive undesired prerequisites, I suggest seriously considering the idea of still taking only those classes you are interested in. It is true that you won't be able to get a diploma this way, but it isn't like you need the degree to get a job!

Universities: Universities excel in their graduate programs. Perhaps you did study English as an undergrad, but then went immediately into the business world. Maybe you always wished you had been able to go on with your studies of Elizabethan poetry instead. If that is the case, then now might be the perfect time to consider taking the more specialized route of a master's or even a Ph.D. A master's is only a one-to three-year commitment full time. A Ph.D. is potentially another two to three years. Reading and writing on a specific topic for one to six years sounds like torture to me, but if your level of interest is that strong, I bet it sounds wonderful to you. And don't be disheartened if you did not take sufficient (or any) classes in your chosen area as an undergrad – not all graduate schools require previous studies in their area. Many schools even offer special intensive undergraduate-level classes that enable people changing careers to "bone up" in areas they didn't study the first time around. From there, you are free to go directly into master's-level classes in your new field. These types of "prep" classes can even turn a past French major into a pre-med in a single year (that is, if your idea of *active* retirement is actually being on-call 72 hours in a row).

Autodidact: The Do-It-Yourself Approach

For many, part of the beauty of an intellectual or artistic pursuit is the time alone. Part of the joy of reading Aristotle is certainly the solitary comfortable recliner, the classical music, and the hot tea at chairside. For others, part of the pleasure comes from the freedom and flexibility such pursuits can afford. A book does not demand you go downtown every Wednesday night for a month to read it; you can read it just as well on the plane to Tibet. A sonata does not demand that you master it by next Tuesday; if you are going skydiving that day, you can wait until Thursday to really get it down. For any person, there are many ways of learning or researching a field.

Reading Lists: If you are not interested in actually attending a college or university, one of the benefits they still can offer are reading lists. Reading lists are compiled by professors for each of their classes and contain all of the books and articles necessary for completion of that class. Obtaining a reading list in your area of interest is like getting an expert to choose all of your books for you. By contacting either the department or the university bookstore directly, you can get reading lists for all the classes for that semester. If not, get a catalog of classes, find a particularly interesting-looking class, and contact the professor directly through his or her department. I bet if you explain to the professor that you are a Wen-Jen who plans on actually going to Greece to do your

Plato readings, he would be happy to give you a copy of his reading list for his seminar on Greek Philosophy.

How-To and Workbooks: Many experts are no more interested in teaching a class than you might be in attending one. Fortunately, a large number of them still feel a need to pass on the knowledge they have acquired in their field. As a result, there are a tremendous number of books out there to help you learn almost any discipline on your own. The key is to find one that really works! This is where specialty bookstores can come in handy. Not only will they assuredly stock the best and widest selection, their staff probably has pretty strong opinions on which books people generally find the most helpful. And if they recommend two or three, why not buy them all? After all, you know what style of learning best suits you, so just select what works best for you from each one.

Another useful resource are the personal reviews that are often attached to books sold on Amazon.com and BN.com (Barnes & Noble). These reviews allow you to get insight into other book users' own experiences and to compare their goals to your own. Both sites also list what other purchasers of this book have bought recently. For example, wouldn't it be helpful to know that the other book being widely purchased by this book's readers is *Suzanne Somers' 365 Ways to Change Your Life*? We all learn differently and for different reasons, and understanding who is behind a review or purchase can be a lot more useful than just "This book is great!"

Lectures and Book Readings – Live and Memorex: Lectures are a wonderful way of staying on top of an area of interest. A live lecture or reading offers the advantages of both the event itself and the question and answer period afterward. They are also good places to meet other people with similar interests or to speak briefly with the lecturers themselves.

Public and college radio stations often broadcast live or taped lectures. Taped lectures are also available at libraries, bookstores, and through such companies as The Teaching Company (1-800-TEACH12), which offers taped lectures from professors from top universities. Lectures on tape have the distinct advantage of allowing one to listen to and review parts of the lecture again and again. They also make wonderful travel companions – you can be listening to a lecture on

Mozart while you are taking the train to catch the opening night of Don Giovanni at Salzburg.

Computer Programs: There are more and more CDs appearing every day for home instruction. But beyond mere learning materials, there is now software available that can enable you to accomplish your desired task with greater ease than ever before. There is software that can allow you to compose music, to edit video clips into small films, to publish your own magazine or newsletter, even to design your own art. And many of these programs are designed for the "consumer" – meaning you don't have to be an expert in the field to successfully use them. For example, if you are writing your first novel or screenplay there is software that will actually take you through the plotting of a story structure step by step (though, unfortunately, it still cannot make you sit down and do the actual writing each day). With tools like these, many goals can be accomplished that might otherwise have seemed out of reach to someone who didn't want to become a full-time student again.

Libraries: Of course you know how to use a library. I just want to point out that there are libraries beyond the one down on Main Street. College and university libraries are filled with books you could never find in the "Adult Fiction" section. Individual departments such as Art, Business, Law, and Medicine often have their own libraries as well. State libraries abound with information that can fill a researcher's days with glee. And finally, the Library of Congress gets larger every single day (and can be browsed through at http://catalog.loc.gov/). Fortunately, many of these libraries offer book-borrowing privileges, even if you're not a registered student or government employee. If not, they do at least allow you to browse. So go, browse, and then with the ISP number in hand, buy yourself a copy. You wanted to check it out for more than two weeks anyway.

Magazines, Trades, and Journals: There is no reason that just because you are not a "professional" in your new area that you shouldn't stay connected with what professionals are saying and doing. Not only do publications in your area of interest offer an opportunity for education but they are also the best place to find notices for additional resources in your new field. If you are new to your pursuit and aren't even sure what journals are available to you, a specialty bookstore in your area of interest will stock a fair amount, or their staff will be able to fill you in.

Even if you are taking your intellectual or artistic journey alone, it is stimulating to be a part of the larger community in this very simple way.

Going Abroad: One of the best ways to learn is to experience things directly for yourself. If you are studying art history, there is no better way than going to see the art itself. With guidebook in hand and rented museum lecture tape and earphones on your head, there isn't much better a place to learn about the history of painting than the Louvre. Why not stroll the streets of James Joyce's Dublin or read Hemingway in his favorite Paris café. Actual experience certainly sheds a light on a topic that even the best lecture and slide show back home could never compete with.

Internet Newsgroups, User Groups, Bulletin Boards, and Chats: The Internet isn't just about news, the market, and E-Bay. An entire world of people out there are having interesting conversations via the Web. Newsgroups, User Groups, Bulletin Boards, and chat groups have been formed around almost any interest you could possible have. By finding a Web page related to your area of interest or by searching through the newsgroups, you could find a lively source of peer conversation, education, and resources on your intellectual topic of choice. More often than not, chats or newgroups break off into private correspondences that can be some of the richest sources of information and companionship on your intellectual journey. These relationships can be wonderfully flexible. Though chats are generally done on a "live" basis, news, user groups, and bulletin boards allow you to correspond or jump in on a topic at any time. Postings usually stay on the board for at least several days and can be responded to at any time. Which means if you are especially keen on the private hour of 4 AM, it is yours to commune in.

Let the Learning Begin!

Regardless of what method (or methods) best suit you, the issue should no longer be "how" but rather when and where. If you have decided to take the learning into your own hands, you must schedule it in and around your other Kaneka plans. If you have decided that classes are the way to go, you should be able to find an appropriately sized program in your area that meets your schedule, flexibility, and mobility. If you find this not to be the case (or you simply desire to study abroad) and you are single – well then the world is your oyster! Go out there and get exactly what you are looking for, wherever it might be! If you are partnered, well then as usual, the world will be your very well negotiated plan. But in any case, the point remains – you now have tools to find what you need, so now is the time to schedule your learning!

Summing Up

Intellectual and Artistic Pursuits are some of the most important arenas that open up to you through your Kaneka transition. They give a value to life that nothing else can replace. To ensure that they become a successful addition to your own life, I suggest the following:

1. Understand and assess your continued needs for information, instruction, and companionship in your Kaneka pursuit.
2. Determine your exact goal.
3. Find an educational approach or program that will enable you to achieve that goal. It must incorporate your desired mode of learning, your schedule, and your desired location for study.
4. Schedule your learning around or in combination with your other Kaneka plans.
5. Get going! All the good stuff lies ahead!

There is only one journey: going inside yourself.
~ Rainer Maria Rilke ~

In ancient China, it was an ideal that at a certain point in one's life one would become a Wenjen[1], stepping away from one's career and turning one's energy toward higher-minded "cultural" pursuits. Given the importance the ancient Chinese placed on culture, a Wenjen's pursuits would have been considered "spiritual" by Chinese standards, because they bring a Wenjen closer to the "higher" things in life. For those people whose idea of spirituality has more to do with a journey inward toward self, or outward toward God, pursuing cultural activities probably would not be a sufficient expression of their ideal.

In ancient India one was expected to develop one's spirituality in the third stage of life. "When a man sees that he is wrinkled and gray, and he sees the children of his children, then he should take himself to the forest."[2] There the person transitioned into the third stage – that of "the forest dweller" – a spiritual seeker and devotee who spends his remaining active years in the forest living a life dedicated to an inward spiritual journey.

Of course, a spiritual journey is just one path among many that an Active-Retiree can choose. And as a true Wenjen you are free to spend your time on any pursuit that beckons you. However, if you find that, like the ancient people of India, you finally have the time to take a spiritual journey, there is no reason that your new Chen-Tao[3] can't ramble "through the spiritual forest" on the way to your other Big List goals.

Spirituality – Different Things for Different People

What you consider "spiritual" will depend largely on who you are. For the ancient Indians it meant an ascetic life of meditation in the forest and dedication to the Vedas. For people in the Judeo-Christian tradition, it could mean participating in functions hosted by their religious organizations or participating in religious studies or joining a contemplative order. However, for many people, spirituality is not

---

[1] Wenjen: A path that is cut and defined by one's own heartfelt goals.
[2] The Laws of Manu.
[3] "Chen-Tao": The right life path for you.

expressed through an organized religion at all, but through an exploration of things that give them a feeling of connection with "the spiritual world." This could mean a myriad of things – meditation, yoga, creative visualization, past-life regression, and the list goes on and on. Finally, there are those for whom the word "spirituality" represents a journey of self-exploration – more of a communion with one's own life than with some outer being or situation. These people find a spiritual connection to life through such activities as traveling, journalizing, and physical exertion. In the end there is no correct way of defining a spiritual journey. Rather, like all things along your Chen-Tao, this journey should reflect who you truly are.

The success of your spiritual journey will come only by properly identifying what you specifically desire from such an endeavor. Therefore, as I have done with all your Kaneka[4] goals, I am now going to ask you to make your goals for this journey more specific. How? By making a list of course! List what you would like to accomplish during your time spent traveling through "the forest."

Beware of judging your list by someone else's definition of "spiritual." "A better understanding of myself" or "greater peace" is just as valid on this list as "a greater connection with God" or "finding a guru." This is about *your* spiritual journey. So go ahead, finish the following sentence: "During my time spent traveling through the forest, I would like to..."

1. _____

2. _____

3. _____

Now that you know what you want, you must determine, as always, how to get it. I realize that many religions or spiritual practices do not find much value in practices other than their own, and in this chapter, I do not attempt to comment on anyone's chosen path. Rather, just as I

---

[4] Kaneka: a rebirth into Active-Retirement (traditionally taking place at age 60).

will do in Chapter 8: "Travel in the External World," I will suggest resources for traveling the world within.

The Quest for the Self

The classic ancient Indian prescription for a forest dweller was to engage in "the Quest for Self." This Hindu practice used fasting and solitude to stimulate inward contemplation. There are other, more modern ways to accomplish similar quests for self.

Travel

For some people, the purpose of travel is as much to gain knowledge of oneself as it is to gain knowledge of the outside world. This kind of travel generally involves destinations dedicated to the mind and spirit rather than to Club Med–like activities. If you find that travel allows you to discover aspects of yourself that you otherwise find difficult to access, perhaps a trip (or trips) planned for this purpose would be in order.

What destinations might stimulate your mind? What type of travel might put you in a situation that inspires contemplation of the larger issues in life? I found that some of my most "spiritual" times came when walking in a forest, trekking in the mountains, or bicycling along a stretch of coast (sans traffic). My mind reached an altered state and looked in on itself. I found these moments enlightening and insightful.

Given the availability of exotic or adventurous travel options and privately designed tours, it is now possible to custom design a tour that both inspires exploration of the inward mind and stimulates interest in the outside world. Great Web sites for this include www.newagetravel.com and www.healthytravel.com.[5]

Outward Bound and Physical Challenges

Most athletes will tell you that the most difficult battles of their sport are fought in the mind. Few activities offer as much insight into one's own psyche as those that entail hardship and physical challenge. Non-professional athletes can gain this same insight by participating in retreats set up to both challenge all levels of physical endurance and

---

[5] www.sacredjourneys.com is a wonderful site that designs spiritual travels just for women.

build character. You can check out www.outwardbound.org to get information on the most well known of these groups. Some groups are geared toward seniors, couples, or women (check out Women's Quest Fitness Retreats at 303/545-9295). Others are specifically designed to incorporate a deliberate "spiritual" aspect or are geared toward a specific type of personal growth.

Get onto www.retreatsonline.com/guide/wilderness.htm for a comprehensive listing of wilderness retreats offered in the United States and Canada.

Vision Quest

Vision Quest is a Native American practice that has become available to everyone. Workshops and retreats abound that safely allow non–Native Americans to partake in a fascinating combination of fasting, meditation, dream work, and survivalism. The fundamental idea is that the combination of fasting and solitary unmapped hiking forces one to face oneself and one's place in the world.

Two Web sites to start with are The Great Round Desert Vision Quests: (www.monitor.net/~circle/vision.htm) and The Earth Rise Foundation (www.bestweb.net/~jos/earthrise/ quests.htm), which offer men-only and women-only quests.

Time Alone or "Going Thoreau"

Sometimes the best thing we can do to better understand ourselves is to take a little time alone. I have known people who have scheduled ten days alone in an isolated cabin and others who have spent a weekend hiking alone to distant springs. Many of them have spoken of the initial fear that sinks in after the first day. At first they are actually afraid of being alone – not so much for personal safety reasons but for fear being left to their own thoughts. Soon the fear gives way to a deep peace that can rarely be found in the company of others. It is a powerful way of accessing a deeper truth about oneself and one's universe.

Journal Writing

One of the ways many "self-help" or inspirational authors (including me) encourage people to come to greater self-knowledge is through journalizing. You are already participating in this process with your

Kaneka Journal, but other types of journal writing are equally effective in their own ways.

An excellent Web site offering information, support, exercises, and ideas about journalizing is: http://www.journals.about.com/arts/journals. Virtually any type of journal writing can be researched there.

Standard Journalizing: With your Kaneka Journal you are engaging in the mind dump of morning journalizing. In contrast, standard journalizing is usually done at day's end. Whereas morning journalizing fosters interaction with the subconscious, evening journalizing deals more with the organizational and thematic functions of the conscious mind. A summation of your daily events can help you to come to terms with your life as well as articulate themes and issues that illuminate and clarify your life. For exploring all the possibilities of standard journalizing, www.writingthejourney.com offers an online journal writing workshop and free monthly newsletters to inspire you along your way.

Travel Journalizing: Many people find that travel puts them in a uniquely contemplative frame of mind. The juxtaposition of one's habitual thoughts against new cultures and landscapes creates a fertile ground for self-exploration and discovery. Keeping a travel journal also serves to document your travels, providing insight into what factors will make for more or less promising travel scenarios in the future. The history of and models for travel journalizing are also available at About.com's Travel Journal page at:

www.journals.about.com/arts/journals/msub29trav.htm.

Dream Journals and Dream Work: You do not have to engage a Jung or Freud to find insight into your dreams. Dream journals, dream workshops, and dream workbooks help you to tap into this untapped third of one's day as a key to understanding the rest of your day. Keeping a regular account of your dreams[6] will bring you closer to the "secret" recesses of your mind, regardless of which psychiatric philosophy you ascribe to. Start with the Web sites www.hyperion.advanced.org/11189/gather/nfjournal.htm,

---

[6] If you do not regularly remember your dreams, most dream workbooks or sites will offer exercises for successfully developing this ability.

www.dreamemporium.com/dream_journal.html,   as   well   as www.heard.org/education/rain/language5/dream.html.

About.com's   Dream   Journal   page   (www.journals.about.com/ arts/journals/msub9drm.htm) lists a dictionary of dream symbolism.

Autobiography

I have worked and I have found it to be quite fruitful. However, unless you have a clear idea of how to tackle this feat, I wouldn't recommend attempting it on your own. Instead, many courses and books are available to guide you on this fascinating journey. In fact, the site www.mystorywriter.com offers software that enables you to effectively write your own life story. An autobiography should not be a chronicle of time but rather a chronicle of events. Try to make it interesting to others and it will become interesting to you. Write of yourself as a character portrait, dig into your memory to remember what you had thought you had forgotten and put on paper those embarrassing moments that are part of everyone's life. Autobiographical writing is a very enjoyable and creative activity.

Creativity and Self-Exploration

Art therapy is a relatively new form of self-exploration. For those people who are not attracted to words (or words alone), art therapy offers some of the same benefits as the writing disciplines.   As your unconscious mind releases images and forms from your life experiences, you can capture them on canvas or in clay. This turns the subconscious into a tangible world from which you can study and gain self-knowledge. Art therapy, however, is not the same as simply making art. To get the full benefit of this type of self-exploration, you should engage a qualified art therapist (yes, they give actual degrees in this area now) or attend an art class led by such a therapist.

The Creativity Workshop (www.creativityworkshop.com) meets in locations around the world and offers exercises in writing, drawing, photography, mapmaking, storytelling, and guided visualization. Another good site, "Windows and Doorways: An Intuitive Creativity Workshop" can be found at: www.allaboutretreats.com/directory.html.

Retreats

Many people enjoy the freedom of leaving their world behind and immersing themselves in an environment geared entirely toward the furthering of their spiritual goals. Whether these goals are as general as making time to meditate on the beauty of nature or as specific as spending a week on raising "emotional awareness," a retreat can be invaluable. The gift of time spent with experts who fully support your spiritual goals can be a powerful catalyst toward spiritual growth. One excellent site is Retreats Online (www.retreatsonline.com).

If you are looking for a retreat to cure what ails you –soul-wise anyway – a little research in this area might do the trick. Perhaps that yoga/chanting/world-dance retreat is exactly the thing you are looking for. What are the credentials of the retreat leaders and organization? Take the time to find out. Nothing could be less enlightening than spending a week with bad food, bad beds, and bad guidance. An example of a good personal development and spiritual retreat is The Hoffman Institute at www.hoffmaninstitute.org (if its program appeals to you). Its staff is well trained in the spiritual arts and it features beautiful spas in natural settings.

Fasting and Silence

If you spend any time researching the major religions and minor ones for that matter, you will repeatedly come across prescriptions for fasting and silence. Mystics, shamans, teachers, and searchers in almost every spiritual discipline across the world and through time have used these tools as keys to accessing the spiritual world.

These practices, however, generally need to be done in retreat. Fasting while spending your day doing other activities doesn't make for much energetic progress. Silence is impossible if any member of your family is able to reach you by fax, phone, modem, or bellow. So if you are drawn to this simple practice, find a retreat center that is set up to accommodate your desires. There are plenty. Just make sure you find the ones that are geared more toward spiritual progress than weight loss.

The Quest for a "Teacher"

Some people avoid the major organized religions but are still attracted to the idea of following someone who has insights and spiritual experience beyond their own.   Throughout history there have been individuals with such great insight into the spiritual realm that they are now considered to be spiritual teachers or "gurus." If this type of guidance appeals to you, Active-Retirement is a great time to find the teacher that suits you.

The Quest for the "Way"

Some people are not looking for a teacher but rather for "a way": a practice that will give them access to a greater spirituality in their life. Meditation, yoga, pranayama, and tai chi all are spiritual practices that can be learned, studied, mastered, and practiced as ways to reach self, God, or enlightenment (whatever floats your particular spiritual boat). Here are a few well-known practices.

Meditation

People of many different spiritual paths worldwide practice meditation. Some claim there is only one correct form of meditation (and of course theirs is it), some say there are 32 forms, some 108. But if you look on the Internet, there must be many times more. Meditation sites abound, and meditation classes are now offered at Zen Centers, Buddhist Centers, Yoga Centers, and Community Centers everywhere. Each has a different focus, sometimes based on a world religion (Zen Buddhism, Hinduism) or sometimes on a worldview.   However, all meditation is about a state of inner peace and connection with self and the universe (God, too, if you want that). Meditation retreats are also offered all over the world, from Nepal to Chicago to Costa Rica, so that you can travel and "aum"[7] all at the same time!

Yoga

What most people refer to as "yoga" is really just the "asana" or physical positions of Yoga. Yoga is not a type of movement but rather a heading for an entire group of physical and spiritual practices. This is

---

[7] A Sanskrit word meaning "the sum total of the universe," which is commonly repeated during meditation.

why you will hear yoga fans comparing the benefits of "Iyengar" and "Hatha" and "Ashtanga" yoga. Yoga Site's (www.yogasite.com) page on yoga styles is an excellent place to research a style to suit your desired outcomes. However, be careful! Yoga, though gentle, is firm. It is best done under the watchful eye of a qualified teacher in a classroom, not on television, video, or the Net.

Pranayama

The other side of Yoga is breathing. Pranayama is a breathing practice that is a basic partner to all of the physical yoga styles (or "asanas"). Often yoga classes will focus on the physical postures, leaving out these equally important breathing exercises. The basic tenet of Pranayama is that the life force or "prana" is channeled through light and the breath, which brings greater spirit, life energy and connection to God to those who practice.

Qi Gong and Tai Chi

When many people think of these practices they think of groups of elderly Chinese slowly moving through peaceful movements of health and meditation. Qi Gong (or Chi Kung as some write it) and Tai Chi Chuan (or Tai Ji Quan) are actually forms of martial arts. However, as such, they fall under a category of exercises called Nui Kong – literally "Inner Cultivation." This large category of Chinese "inner" martial arts[8] involves the practice of standing, sitting, moving, static, and even dreaming exercises, all for the purpose of channeling and directing "Qi" (or "Chi") – the life force or life energy – through the body with the goal of attaining harmonious existence in all situations. Correct balance of one's Qi energy brings peace and health to the mind and the body.

The Quest for God

Many of us already have a religion that has served us well for many years. Active-Retirement can be good time to get more involved with that religion. However, now that you have the time for contemplation, make sure that you are on the spiritual journey that is right for you. Perhaps the religion that satisfied your needs as a working person all

---

[8] Including Ba Kua (Pa Gua) and Hsing I (Xing Yi).

these years will not be the right one to "go into the spiritual forest" with. If you find that you have outgrown the spiritual group you presently attend, it is no crime to consider changing. That's what Kaneka is about.

Mine, Yours, or Mom & Dad's

Maybe you were an active and loyal participant in your chosen faith all your life. Maybe you never "chose" your faith at all, but rather followed the footsteps of your parents by continuing to practice the faith in which they raised you. Or maybe you have simply felt the pull toward religion but never had enough time to find the group that would meet your spiritual needs.

Looking East

Most of us in the West have been raised in the Judeo-Christian tradition of "organized religion" and "God" and "being good." Our culture as a whole says very little about the tenets of Buddhism, Zen Buddhism, Taoism, or other spiritual practices from Asia and the East. Many people are beginning to find new spiritual homes in these Eastern alternatives, which have very different spiritual practices and philosophies from those of their mom and dad's old church or temple.

Visit the Holy Lands

If you feel that you have found your "spiritual home" already, Active-Retirement can still spice things up. This is the perfect phase of life for travel that is related to the history and sites of one's faith or practice. Visiting the lands that the teachers, saints, holy people, and prophets have walked can be a life-changing experience.[9] For some people, visiting a religious historical site offers the insight into and perspective of a spirituality that words alone could never bring. Religious traditions also have prescribed pilgrimages that deepen one's commitment and relationship to one's faith. Whatever reason you find for travel within your spiritual practice, Active-Retirement affords the perfect opportunity for which to do it.

---

[9] www.newagetravel.com is a wonderful place to start planning such a trip.

Summing Up

Active-Retirement is the time to embark on a spiritual or inner journey. To make yours most successful, I would suggest the following:

1. Clarify and list three goals for your "time spent traveling through the forest."
2. If your spiritual quest is for self-knowledge, research and consider how you can use the tools of travel, physical challenges, time alone, journal writing, and other methods to realize your goal.
3. If your desire is to find a spiritual teacher, use the Web, New Age bookstores, and local lectures to find a spiritual teacher that appeals to you.
4. If you are searching for more of a spiritual "practice," look into meditation, yoga, or tai chi as examples of long-held traditions for reaching a higher state in body and mind.
5. If you are more inclined toward spiritual practices with a strong philosophy behind them, try exploring some of the Eastern traditions.

*We are all guilty of crime, the great crime of not living life to
the full. But we are all potentially free. We can stop thinking
of what we have failed to do and do whatever lies within our
power.*
~ Henry Miller ~

*Certainly, travel is more than the seeing of sights;
it is a change that goes on, deep and permanent,
in the ideas of living.*
~ Miriam Beard ~

Why Do We Travel?

To some, travel represents the opportunity for a different, freer
existence.

For others, encountering diverse peoples and cultures helps them
alter their view of their current life and experiences.

The idea of travel can be an extension of our childhood dreams of
adventures in faraway lands. The return to adventure can represent a
reawakening of childlike joys and the basic miracles of life.

Travel can be a means to understanding oneself better as an adult.
Perhaps by traveling back to the place of one's birth (where everything
seems so small) or to the birthplace of one's parents or ancestors, a
deeper meaning can be brought to one's life. Travel helps some people
reach a better understanding of who they are.

There are others for whom "travel" means something completely
different. Upon hearing the above definitions, some would say, "If that's
travel, I don't want to travel, I want to go [skiing, scuba diving, trekking,
art-viewing, etc.]". But their definition is just as valid. They are merely
"single-purpose" travelers whose sole purpose for traveling is to enjoy
one particular activity.

When I was interviewing people who were on the verge of Kaneka,
my first question was always, "What do you want to do after you retire?"
Almost without exception they answered, "I want to travel more."
When I asked if that meant they wanted to get on a cruise ship and just
sail around the globe, they would always say, "No, I want to go to

_____!" Everyone knew exactly where he or she wanted to go and what he or she wanted to do there.

We say we just want to "travel." But if pressed, we know exactly where, what, and how we want to do it. Trip planning is merely a natural extension of these desires. It starts with deciding what you want to do and continues by your researching those goals and deciding on the best ways of accomplishing them. There is no need to get overwhelmed by all the possibilities of "travel." Travel means different things to different people. Since I am sure you already have a good idea of what type of travel you want to do and where you want to do it, I will simply offer you some guidance before making your plans.

Where Do We Travel?

Spending a month in Paris is very different from traveling the migratory path of the FooFoo bird along the Amazon River. Different types of travel bring up different concerns.

Of course, the type of trip you want to take will determine the specifics of how you should research it, but there are some set avenues you can follow in order to drum up information on any style of traveling.

Travel Bookstores: The advent of travel bookstores has made researching trips a wonderful one-stop-shopping experience. In fact it is hard to leave a travel bookstore without having ideas for several additional trips. These stores have books ranging from highly specialized trips (the best Rocky Mountain treks to take with a dog) to generalized regional ones (Italy).

Guidebooks: Travel bookstores are a great place for gathering your guidebooks. There are lots of good guidebooks out there, and choosing the right one depends a lot on the type of trip you want to take. Here are my takes on some of the better known ones:

Time Out in [Name Your City]: one of the best for theaters and shopping, or if you plan on living in a city for an extended period of time.

Fodor: very thorough and quite accurate at giving ratings for good hotels and restaurants.

Frommer's: reads a little better than most and lists the "top ten" sights of a city. I have always found this guidebook to be very useful, especially when one has limited time in a city. My wife and I usually choose only a few of the top ten sights as there are always some we are less interested in, then we can spend more time pursuing them in depth.

Eyewitness: marvelously detailed with lots of pictures.

Rough Guides: Forget about it. Just look at the title – it's not for you.

Your best bet when trying to find the right guidebook is to choose three or four different books and compare their descriptions of one important place. Then check out the shops, restaurants, museums, and hotels each book lists in the locale. If there is also a particular activity you are interested in, compare each guidebook's coverage on that area of interest. By the end of this process, it should be pretty clear which books are speaking to you and which are not. However, you might find that one book simply doesn't cover it all. Then don't be afraid to buy two or three. You are going to be spending a lot of money on this adventure, so finding something you want to do or see or getting a good hotel is worth a lot more than the extra $25 spent on another guidebook. On the other hand, do take the time to narrow it down to just two or three, as you don't want to be dragging thirty pounds' worth of guidebooks across Egypt either.

The old-fashioned type bookstore: Travel doesn't just mean "moving around". It is history, culture, language, art, sport, adventure – you name it. Therefore, doing some old-fashioned reading about what interests you the most might help you define what you want to accomplish during your trip. Are you interested in exploring your family history? Then a book on researching family trees might be good background. Do you want to ski in the Swiss Alps? Then perhaps reading up on skiing in Europe would give you some information you need. History of the Samurai fascinates you? Then certainly you should do some intensive historical research before you commit to your final itinerary. Regardless of your interest, taking the time to read up on it will only add to your appreciation of your travels and wet your appetite for the trip itself.

The ever-present Web! The Web offers both the travel research opportunities of a travel bookstore and the subject research opportunities of a traditional bookstore. It is also home of many sites that offer information and opportunities that can't be found anywhere else:

Expedia (www.expedia.com): A self-serve, online travel agency. Make flight, car, cruise, and hotel – even golf course reservations all over the world. You can also find street maps of the United States and Europe.

Travelocity (www.travelocity.com): Another self-service, online travel agency – but beyond just plane reservations, you can look at a floor plan of the plane and choose your actual seat online. Additional perks include (among other things) a search engine for bed-and-breakfasts, a weather center and a U.S. currency exchange calculator.

United Airlines (www.ua.com): United Airlines' site offers you access not only to its national and international "e-fares" and vacation packages but also to flight information, price, and itinerary comparisons with all other airlines. The United site will even allow you to purchase tickets directly from the other airlines if you decide that one of their flights appeals to you more than a United flight. The Net is an easy way to shop and compare airfare across the board.

American Airlines (www.aa.com): American Airlines' Web site offers both "webfares" and "netsavers" discounts that are available only on tickets purchased over the Web.

City Search (www.citysearch.com): A search engine that allows you to find information on movies, entertainment, events, and nightlife in most U.S. and some European cities. Search from keywords to specific types of listings (such as restaurants – "bagels," "brewpubs," and "Cajun"). You can find detailed descriptions of establishments, times, and prices as well as directions and local road maps.

Elderhostel (www.elderhostel.org): This site combines education, world travel information, and an opportunity to make new friends with other adventure-minded seniors. This 25-year-old nonprofit organization has many learning adventure trips. Its excellent Web site has a full catalog of trips and trip registration forms.

Spa Finder (www.spafinder.com): Search engine for finding spas off all kinds, worldwide. Choose a type of spa program from such areas as supreme pampering, fasting, most challenging workout, gambling nearby, or cross-country skiing.

Hideaways (www.hideaways.com): This search engine allows one to find first-class villas all over the world and the private, romantic, or "hidden" getaway.

How Do We Travel?

Ultimately, travel is about moving. Therefore, the methods of travel we choose will very much determine the experience we will have.

Flying

The first step of your trip usually involves flying to a destination. You can then choose your method of travel within your destination. You might choose to fly, depending on the conditions of the roads and the internal transportation system. However, when you fly on a "National Airline" you might not get the same level of service or cleanliness that you get on U.S. and international airlines. I have flown with goats and chickens (Air Guatemala), with broken seats and overhead bins that don't close (Air India), and with a doorway that was tied closed by a rope (Air Ethiopia).

Commercial Bus

Special first-class buses, in certain select destinations, do exist. In some countries, such as Switzerland and Norway, there are numerous acceptable bus trips. In general bus travel on anything but a tour-chartered bus (which is designed for western bodies) is something you generally want to avoid. If you find yourself considering the bus as an option, at least be aware of what "first class" means in different areas of the world. In Mexico, a first-class bus means one whose interior might be swathed in red velveteen and tassels but whose seats are still tiny and cramped. You might not realize that the bus lacks a bathroom until the driver tells you that it won't be making a scheduled stop for another ten hours. Also the bus drivers in most of Central and South America are world famous for driving so recklessly around mountain passes that unless you are into travel strictly for the "adventure" aspect, I can guarantee that you will experience far more terror than pleasure.

In other words, beware, be careful, and be well informed before traveling by bus.

Trains

They are excellent trains in some parts of the world. In Europe, Japan, and South Africa you can get wonderful, clean and on time trains. A first-class sleeper car along the Nile can be one of the most pleasant ways to get a real sense of Egypt. However, make sure you always do your research. I would generally avoid taking trains unless they have true first-class sleeper berths or other special accommodations. Your guidebooks should be able to give you some idea. Train rides can be long, and unpleasant ones longer. The three days I spent on the Trans-Siberian Express felt more like a sentence in Siberia than a scenic journey through it.

Drive Yourself

This used to be my favorite method of travel. It requires a strong sense of adventure and good map-reading ability. (I had a real problem trying to read the street signs in Russia). I have generally given up the concept of renting a car and driving myself when traveling in the more remote places. Since I almost had a major mishap on a back mountain road in Ecuador, involving an oil truck, a tropical storm and a car whose alternator was dying, leaving our jeep without lights. If you do rent a car, make sure that you have good insurance coverage. Everyone knows all Americans are rich (you are), and that they can be sued for a lot of money.

Hiring a Car with a Driver

This is a very comfortable way to travel, and it often doesn't cost much more than the price of the car rental. There is the cost for the driver, his food, and lodging; but don't worry, he doesn't stay at the five-star hotels with you. Some hotels even have special rooms for drivers. This type of travel gives you a lot of flexibility, but be sure to specify that your car have heat and air-conditioning (if available).

Cruises

There are a number of advantages to taking a cruise. The biggest one is that you are in one location and don't have to unpack your suitcases every day. You also know there will be plenty of good food, that the people will speak your language, and that there will be entertainment.

The negative factors are the flip side of the positive ones. You will get too much food (and little of the authentic local cuisine); you will have little to no real contact with the actual people of the country; instead, you will be herded like cattle into small boats to go ashore, usually to a group of vendors selling tacky souvenirs, and your focus will continually be redirected back to the ship rather than to the country you are visiting. All that being said, there are still a lot of good things about cruising.

If you are going on a cruise,[1] make sure it is a top-ranked cruise line, get a nice cabin, and don't feel obligated to become friends with everyone on the boat. And finally, just because the food is paid for, don't feel you have to eat it all.

There are also a series of "boutique" cruise ships, which carry fewer than a hundred passengers and often go to unique or exotic locales. I know of cruises that travel to the Antarctic, the Amazon River, Alaska, Papua New Guinea, and other little-visited areas. The ship may even carry a naturalist or someone who specializes in the region being visited. These boats combine luxury travel with adventure travel, and just might be the best of both worlds.

With Whom Do We Travel?

One of the most important (and most difficult) decisions in travel is choosing one's travel partners – for they are the people, who can make or break your trip.

Tours: A Bevy, a Group, or a Herd?

The most common way to travel is with a tour group (though you are not a common person). There are all types and levels of tours. You've probably already been on some tours that you've enjoyed and others that

---

[1]If you are prone to seasickness, have your doctor talk to you about the various pills and patches that are currently available.

were less than satisfactory. Here are some guidelines on how to find a tour that's good for you.

References from friends – *who have the same taste and travel habits as you do.* I once followed the reference of a friend whose main pride in life was finding the cheapest tour for any itinerary. I ended up traveling with thirty-four German students and a tour guide who had never visited the country we were touring. Plus I had to help change a tire on the bus.

The number of people on the tour. This is a key factor. It is possible for forty Japanese tourists to travel in a group, for they will follow instructions, cue up, and be on time. However forty Americans, unless they are elementary school teachers, are a disaster. We are a country of individuals who usually obey the law (except for illegal U turns) and sometimes follow instructions. I believe that fifteen is a maximum number for a group, with twelve being better and eight being near perfect.

A bevy of travelers in a group tour.

Hotels. Identify what hotels have been booked for the tour and where are they located. Check the hotels against their descriptions in one your guidebooks. Be watchful of words like quaint, charming, old-fashioned, intimate, etc. Our ancestors were much smaller than we are. Also watch for "just a few minutes from the center of the city" (maybe by helicopter). You are not traveling out of the country to sightsee a hotel. After a hard day of sightseeing you will need a comfortable bed, a hot shower, a tub to soak your feet in, your bed turned down, and a chocolate on your pillow. A concierge who can get you the tickets you need, as well as a *USA Today* or *The New York Times* in the morning, is also very welcome. I recommend a four-star hotel. Its price will be higher but it will help you enjoy your trip. A $3.00 cold Diet Coke from a mini-bar after a hot day sightseeing the Taj Mahal really tastes quite marvelous.

Tour leaders. Check out the leaders of the tour. From their bio do they sound like someone you want to spend two weeks with? Does he or she speak good English or are they like the Korean guide we once had where I had to translate everything for my wife? Not that he didn't speak English or that I understood Korean, but his sentence structure fit my knowledge of German syntax much better than it did my wife's American English.

Local guides. Are you going to have local guides in addition to your leader or will your leader be the "expert" telling you about each of the 27 different countries you will be visiting over your 14-day trip. Local experts are one of the best parts of a well-organized tour.

27 Countries in 14 Days?!? In reality my wife and I found that the fewer countries we visited and the fewer number of times we had to change hotels, the more we enjoyed our trip. At least three days per hotel was optimal.

Method of transportation. Would you take a twelve-hour bus ride in the United States? If not, should you have to take one in a place where an alternative is possible? In Bhutan it is not, in France it certainly is. If your transportation is a minivan, find out what type of van it is and how many people are going to be in it. Most Japanese minivans are too small for Westerners – especially too many Westerners.

What kind of group do you want to tour with? There are many specialized tours hosted by museums, archeological groups, universities, and even antique-buying groups. They all sound very fascinating but after you've visited the tenth 12th century gothic church and noted that the windows on this one are larger than the ones back on number seven, you may decide you should have chosen a more generalized tour. One key way to obtain needed details about a tour is to have an in-depth discussion with someone who has already been on that tour or on a similar tour with the same company. In asking your questions you should be very specific: not just, "Did you enjoy the tour?" but ask about the food, accommodations, travel, guides, company of the other travelers, etc.

Specialty travel agencies. Obviously there are many excellent travel agencies out there, but a few specialize in more unique or adventurous tour options than others. If it is specifically the exotic or the adventurous that you are looking for, you might be more satisfied with a tour set up by a travel agency that has those goals specifically in mind. The following is a list of some such agencies that I've had good experiences with:

- <u>Zegrahm Expeditions</u>:[2] Specializes in "eco-expeditions." Treks, hikes, safaris, ships, birding adventures – even submarine travel. Some examples include
  Ethiopia, birthplace of the Blue Nile
  The Titanic – visit it in a submarine!
  Madagascar
  Antarctica
- <u>Immersia Travel</u>:[3] Specializes in culturally immersive travel. From exploring local cuisine while staying in luxury accommodations to sleeping on the floor of a tribal villager's home out in a remote area of the jungle. Some examples:
  The hill tribes of Thailand
  Sulawesi (Indonesia)
  New Guinea
- <u>Butterfield & Robinson</u>:[4] Easy to moderate walking, cycling, rafting and kayaking tours. Full support (you can get into the van anytime). Gourmet food and wonderful accommodations. A real vacation with some exercise. Tours include
  Johnstone Straight: Sea Kayaking with the Orcas
  Bike and Walk from the Great Wall to Tibet's Frontier
  Patagonia: Walking the Wildest Place on Earth
- <u>Abercrombie & Kent</u>[5]: Specializes in high-end exotic vacations of all kinds – from general safaris to individual and family tours. Some tour name examples:
  Vintage Italy with a performance by Luciano Pavarotti
  Journey Around the World

---

[2] www.zeco.com, 1-800-628-8747.
[3] www.immersiatravel.com, 1-800-207-5454.
[4] www.butterfield.com, 1-800-678-1147.
[5] www.aandktours.com, 1-800-757-5884.

Peru with Machu Picchu at Christmas
In the Footsteps of Famous Artists
- Geographic Expeditions:[6] In between Immersia and Abercrombie & Kent. Cultural and historical tours of the world led by experts. From easy vacations to full trekking.
Festivals of Rajasthan
Frontiers of Inner Asia: The Southern Silk Road
Morocco from Casablanca to Marrakech
- Country Walkers:[7] Worldwide walking vacations – with full support. Truly worldwide tours tailored to individuals, singles, women, families, and adults. Custom and private tours are also available. The perfect speed to really explore the flora and fauna of a region.

With all of these criteria in mind (and all of these options) you should be able to find the tour that best suits your needs.

Traveling with Friends

Some people simply don't like the idea of having to meet, greet, and travel with strangers. Small talk over dinner isn't their idea of relaxation. For them, traveling in a tour group is obviously out. But that doesn't mean that traveling with friends has to be in. In theory, travel with friends sounds wonderful. But many times it simply doesn't work. We lost some of our best friends on a trip, not because they "died climbing Everest," but because at the end of it we weren't talking to each other and couldn't figure out how we'd ever been friends to begin with.

If you do want to take a trip with some friends, take a short trip first and see how it works out. If it doesn't, you will have lost neither your friends nor too much time and money. But if it does work and you do venture a long trip together, remember that it doesn't mean you have to do everything together all of the time. Plan some time on your own and

---

[6] www.geoex.com, 1-800-777-8183.
[7] www.countrywalkers.com, 1-800-464-9255.

some meals by yourself or with other people. It will make the trip better for all of you.

Traveling Alone: The Private Tour

By traveling "alone," I mean traveling alone or with your partner. Not that your partner isn't a friend, but by this point I would hope you were not at risk of losing each other by attempting a trip. Travel can be a challenge, but I'm sure you've mastered harder things before than traveling together.

The first step in creating a private tour is to find a travel agent or agency that specializes in the country or area you want to visit. If you are doing a special kind of travel, such as traveling for scuba, then find an agency that specializes in that sport.

In either case, it is important to check references for the agency or particular agent.   Simply ask for references you can call in order to inquire about past customer satisfaction. This might seem unusual to them, but it shouldn't seem unreasonable.

Once you have found a good agent, you should explain what you want to do, how you want to do it, and at what level you want to do it. Also mention the things that are most important to you, such as air-conditioning, cleanliness, and quiet. Also, it is best at this time to let the travel agent know whether you are planning to use frequent-flier miles for an upgrade or ticket. Then have the agency prepare a preliminary itinerary for you along with estimated costs. The agent will probably want a nonrefundable deposit, but I believe this is a fair exchange for their efforts.

Then take the itinerary and hotel list and compare it to the recommended ones in your guidebooks. I also use the hotels chosen by some of the better tours. (see previous list) This should give you a good idea of whether or not you are on the right track.

A description of a heavenly trip: My wife and I took a trip to the backcountry of Indonesia. We had a wonderful travel agent who knew the country and had her own set of tour guides (this didn't mean they worked exclusively for her, but she generally booked them whenever she had a client or a tour).

We had upgraded our tickets to business class using frequent-flier miles. We took a Lincoln Towncar to the airport, sat in the business-class lounge till the plane took off, and had a relatively pleasant eighteen-hour flight.[8]

On our arrival a driver and a guide met us. The guide spoke good English and really knew the region. As we hopped around the Indonesian islands, at each airport we were met by drivers and guides, each knowing the area in which we were traveling. The hotels were usually the best in the area, and we had flexibility in terms of what we wanted to do. In one place we decided we really didn't want to see another palace, so we took a boat up the river. Another time we wanted to take a walk, so our driver dropped us off at one village and we walked over to another where he picked us up. This type of flexibility can only be had on a private tour.

What Do We Eat While Traveling?

Some Quick Thoughts on Culinary Delights

When you are in a country you probably should try some of the local cuisine. But as I have been getting older, my digestive system does not cooperate so well with spices or certain native specialties. A couple of spoonfuls of Milk of Magnesia or some Pepcid AC taken prior to a meal can coat one's stomach and make it friendlier to exotic foods. But if you are traveling to some highly exotic land, check with your doctor. In some cases there are new prescription medications that might actually prevent "Montezuma's Revenge."

Even so, when you don't want to eat something that is put in front of you, especially if it is still wiggling, there are a number of things you can say that will get you off the hook without offending the host too much. Try, "My doctor has forbidden me to eat fried caterpillars or any other fried insects," or, "I get an allergic reaction to beetle wings in squid juice or really any insect wings in squid juice."

---

[8] An eighteen-hour flight is never pleasant, even with four movies. Two of the movies were bad, but the other two were terrible though they did have Chinese subtitles – which might have helped had we known any Chinese.

Anyway you get the idea. It is better to tell a small fib than to be up half the night with stomach cramps or the runs.

How Do We Survive Travel?

Which brings us to a very important part of travel. Surviving it. There are three ways to successfully survive travel, and they all depend on you.

Medical preparation: In this day and age it is very important to check in with your physician at least a month before extensive travel. Beyond providing you with antibiotics for the road (which are FDA approved) and writing you an additional prescription for those antihistamines you just can't do without, your physician should be able to give you any vaccines or additional medications that might be suggested for the areas to which you are traveling. The hepatitis bugs are very prevalent worldwide – a simple round of vaccinations can make your travels (relatively) worry-free. Furthermore, the proper stomach medicines can help you continue to enjoy that long planned-for trip past just the first few days.[9] But do make sure to check in with your doctor at least four weeks before traveling, as several of the vaccines can require at least one more booster shot before you go.

Documentation, visas, and the law: If you are not traveling with a tour group, make sure you understand the "business" aspects of the countries to which you are planning to travel. A good travel agent should be able to help you secure all the necessary documentation and visas, and give you any additional travel information you need. But it behooves you to be on top of it as well. You don't want to discover your agent's mistake at the Uzbekistan border, because the inside of a gulag isn't the best place to sort out any visa or "exporting" errors. So break out those guidebooks, call any embassies you need to, and make sure you understand everything required to get into the country, how long you will be allowed to stay, and what exactly you can take with you once you leave.

---

[9] I have also found that taking echinacea-goldenseal mixtures to boost the immune system and carrying "Cold-Ease" zinc lozenges to knock out a cold have drastically cut down on those post-plane-flight colds and flus.

Planning for Reality: Getting into a dirty taxi with too many suitcases, standing in line for an hour to check luggage, sitting in sticky seats at the airport while Hare Krishnas try to get donations, and then getting cramped into the middle seat of a plane designed for super models are not a wonderful way to start a trip.

Start with a private car or limousine service, pay for skycaps to check your luggage at the curb, wait for your flight in the airport lounge (business-class international will get you into most lounges), and fly all fourteen hours in business-class seats (by upgrading, buying two for one through Amex-Platinum, or paying full price 'cause it's worth it). Once you arrive, make sure you are met and transferred to your hotel. At the hotel check in, take a shower and a nap and maybe even get a massage to get the kinks out. Now you are ready to start your vacation.

And now you understand the first principle of enjoyable travel – It's worth doing it right. Bon Voyage!

Summing Up

Even though travel means different things to different people, most still agree that they want more of it. But regardless of your specific travel goals, the key to enjoying travel is to do proper research and make realistic, well-informed plans. To that end, I suggest the following:

1. Identify *your* specific goals and interests in traveling.
2. Research the country of your destination and areas of interest by using travel bookstores, guidebooks, regular bookstores, and the Web.
3. Identify modes of travel that will work for your goals (be realistic).
4. Choose your travel companions (or lack thereof) wisely!
5. If choosing to travel with a tour, research the tour thoroughly. Check references from friends and past tour takers. Find out specifically how many people are to be on the tour, the hotels and modes of transportation planned, and the qualifications of the tour leaders and local guides.
6. If you have specialty interests, research specialty tours, which might group you with experts and individuals who have the same type of travel in mind.

7. Visit your doctor to medically prepare for your trip.
8. Make sure you understand all of the legal requirements and ramifications of your travels (and purchases).
9. Be realistic. Travel can be hard – so make it as easy as possible for yourself!

It is seldom that an American retires from business to enjoy his fortune in comfort...he works because he has always worked, and knows no other way.
~ Thomas Nichols ~

You love your job, you do it better than anyone else (really?), and you want to keep working!

Are you sure? Let's examine this for just a moment. You are absolutely positive that you really want to continue full force – working as hard as ever and for as many hours? Yes?!? Then give this book to someone else – and get back to work!

On the other hand, if you feel there are other things you would like to accomplish (yes, the Big List!), if your job no longer fully captivates you, or if the long hours spent doing the work no longer come easily, then maybe it is time to think about Active-Retirement.

Active-Retirement doesn't mean you can't work. Work is a very important part of one's life. It contributes income, structure, identity, social contact, and psychological satisfaction. Active-Retirement implies that you will not be tied to your work for the income because Wenjens don't need the money – they are already affluent.

Another way of looking at this is that for a Wenjen, work no longer needs to be a way of making money but rather a way of making joy. It means that if you desire to keep working after your Kaneka, you won't have to hold a nine-to-five job, get a salary, or even get paid at all. Instead, you are free to be anything you please – be it a passionate volunteer, a landscape painter, or a novelist. It means that you are finally free to pursue any of the paths not taken or any of the new paths that have begun to appeal to you over the years.

Active-Retirement doesn't mean having to make a choice between "working" or enjoying your "leisure." It means enjoying work to the fullest, while still maintaining the freedom to pursue leisure (because golf and skiing still don't qualify as work). For a Wenjen this is easy because the remaining benefits that come with work are all present in your Big List activities. All the structure, identity, and social contact you desire can come through vigorous pursuit of your painting, volunteering, traveling, or whatever Big List goals you have set for yourself. And this lifestyle, built upon the accomplishing of your own dreams and desires, will certainly offer all the psychological satisfaction you could possibly need. It is simply a matter of choosing to pursue your passion as your work! It is that simple!

But I Love My Job!

If you are lucky enough to already have your passion as your work, then the idea of "retiring" might seem very difficult. Some of us feel tied to the positions or areas we are now considering leaving. Many of us have developed skills over the years that bring us great satisfaction, and we do not immediately see any way of exercising those skills outside our present jobs. But Active-Retirement doesn't mean you necessarily have to walk away from a job you love.

There are alternatives.

A Horizontal Move?

Yes, there is a definite shortage of skilled and trained executives. If you are retiring at 55 you probably can find a position at a competitor or in a similar industry. The question is, do you want to start over – even at a high level? If the answer is yes, then my next question is why?

What's your answer? Money? You are already affluent! Prestige? You've already accomplished many wonderful things related to work; isn't it time to move on to the accomplishment of other desired goals? Is it fear? Are you uncomfortable tackling something new? Maybe it's none of the above. Maybe you aren't ready to write a screenplay, compose music, or travel to Tibet next summer.

For argument's sake, I'm going to assume that you really are ready and that you do want to do everything on your Big List. I'm sure we can continue with your Kaneka and find more reasonable ways for you to continue doing the type of work you love.

Consulting

As the country gets grayer and the workplace ages, the talent (that's you) becomes scarce. Consequently, some of the largest consulting and multinational firms are creating innovative programs to retain or attract older employees. Many are offering consulting positions with attractive perks and flexible work hours and days (flextime) to fit your needs. In return, companies get the continuing benefit of your experience. While this might sound like a perfect compromise between continuing your career and pursuing other Big List goals, don't jump until you have all the details and have thought about all the repercussions of this new style of working.

Although not always possible, some Active-Retirees start by consulting for the company they worked for previously. Unfortunately, this can lead to conflict. If you were a CEO or VP with the power to give orders and get things done, it may not be easy to become merely an advisor where people can choose not to listen to your advice. On the other hand, if people happen to listen to it too much, you could also find yourself in conflict with the executive who is currently holding your old position.

There is always the option of consulting for other companies. I tried this route and personally found that it held a lot of the same conflicts that working at my old company would have had. Eventually, I decided I would do better simply breaking with my previous role completely.

Nevertheless, if the idea of consulting appeals to you, you must answer some difficult questions before accepting a new position. You made a list of things that you want to accomplish along your Chen Tao. It is your responsibility now to maintain the time and freedom to accomplish them. Can you assure yourself that you will be able to put aside your work after just three days each week, or will you often be needing to "finish just one more item" on your days off? Remember, consulting is still a long-term commitment of employment to a company. It may appear wonderful compared with your present 80-hour-a-week high-stress position, but will it really take the place of painting the Grand Canyon at sunset or skiing Aspen for three weeks?

Mentoring

Another way of staying in your field but adding some flexibility is mentoring. By mentoring a younger associate, you can continue to utilize your skills and pass on your knowledge to the field but without being directly responsible for projects. Companies such as Chevron, Prudential, and Monsanto are even developing in-house mentoring programs between their retiring and junior employees. Mentoring has the great advantage of working without "deadlines" and time-intensive responsibilities. Someone else does all the detail and time-sensitive work. Although this could invite frustration as you realize that you could do it better and in a much shorter amount of time, mentoring allows you to take that time to do other things – things that you actually might enjoy more or have never had the time to try before.

But Business Is My Life!

Starting Your Own Business

Many Active-Retirees feel that they want to start their own business. Bursting with ideas and having years of experience and mistakes behind them, they know that they can do things better than their previous bosses. Lucky for them, the advent of the computer, fax, and Internet has made it much easier to create and maintain a worldwide business.

The Internet has essentially opened the gates to home-based companies. You no longer need a building, lease, a lot of staff, or major capital to buy inventory. You can take a simple hobby or passion and turn it into a business – be it gardening, collecting earthworms, or specializing in vinyl records from the '30s. With the computer you can create newsletters and e-mail them to niche groups or start your own e-commerce Web site. Or you can develop a new concept and run with it. The opportunities are limitless. Just know that on the Internet, if you find the right niche, you can find yourself competing right along with the big boys.

If you are more inclined toward the local business venture, the initial start-up costs will be much more significant (unless you have been collecting antiques for the last 30 years and now plan on selling off your collection from your garage), but the rules remain essentially the same.

There are four major axioms that you must always remember when starting a business:

1. It will take longer than you think.
2. It will cost more than you budgeted.
3. It will be more difficult than you thought.
4. You will run into major obstacles.

If all of these are acceptable to you, then go to the next step: research to see if the business already exists. It is important that you study what is already available. A large part of creating a successful business is understanding what already exists, in terms of both your competition and the market. This research will also help you understand the amount of work that will be required to start your venture. After the research, reassess whether the task still looks do-able.

That being said, there has never been a better time to start a business than today. It's lots of work, lots of fun, and maybe just what you want to do, but it requires a tremendous amount of time and commitment. I say this not to discourage you but to force you to think. Before you begin your own business you must ask yourself: Is this something that I want as the main focus of my life for the next ten years?

Investing

Perhaps a more manageable way to keep one's hands in business is investing. Though many like to turn their money over to a money manager, you could now make the decision to get more personally involved. Each approach has its advantages, and if one wanted to split the difference, there isn't any reason why one can't, thereby enjoying the pleasure of investing without bearing the entire burden.

Another satisfying way to invest is to do so in "start-up" companies. This can be done as an individual investor or as a group. Studying companies and investing in them can be extremely rewarding. You learn about the trends in the economy and stay abreast of the directions in which business and technology are moving. World events can begin to take on new interest and meaning. Entire areas of knowledge that were previously unknown to you can suddenly become a part of your life.

But whatever you do, be careful. Don't invest in "double your money in six months" schemes. Remember, you are a person of relative affluence. Money is important but not crucial. Earning money through investing is part game and part education, but it is probably not a healthy center of an Active-Retired life.

Board of Directors

Many Active-Retirees have found that being on an advisory board or a board of directors works out quite well for them. This is one activity that I have really enjoyed. It permits me to use my knowledge and skills but requires only one meeting every three months, with a few e-mails and phone calls in between. A board can also keep you current with what is going on in the business world. But you are not limited to serving on the board of your own field or business. The expertise one has gained over the years can be applicable in many areas. Several Active-Retirees I interviewed have enjoyed serving on the boards of arts, education, and charitable nonprofits; becoming involved with the boards and committees in their religious organizations (watch the politics in all); or working on the boards of political and environmental organizations.

Doing "Good" Work

Volunteering

Wenjens are first-class volunteers. You have time and a flexible schedule. You have highly developed skills and an extensive wealth of experience, knowledge, and connections that are priceless to a not-for-profit. For a Wenjen, the question isn't, "Can I be of service?" but simply, "Who would I like to be of service to, and how?"

Who Shall I Help?

Determining who to help or what cause to support is the first step. Are there groups of people you wish to aid? Is there a problem you want to work on? Is there good work being done that you would like to have a hand in furthering? The most important part of your volunteer work is that it is in an area that you feel passionate about. The following is a very broad and preliminary list of charitable interests, just to get your mind working:

General Areas Where Assistance Is Always Needed

People

Artists: Foundations, Funding, Business and Legal Guidance

Children: Education, Healthcare, Mentoring, Day Care, After-School Programs, Summer Programs, Foster Care, Child Abuse, Child Labor, Homelessness

The Elderly: Transportation, Entertainment, Companionship, Home Hospice, Home Service (shopping, pet care, etc.)

Emergency Relief: Victims of Natural Disasters, Wars, Famine, Persecution

The Homeless: Housing, Food, Clothing, Mental Health, Health Care, Shelters

Human Rights: Victims of Persecution, Victims of Human Rights Abuses, Political Prisoners, Child Labor, Forced Labor, Prisoners of War

The Mentally and Physically Handicapped: Job Placement and Training, Transportation, Entertainment, Health Care, Legal Issues

Political Rights: for Children, Women, Migrant Workers, the Sick or Disabled, Animals, Prisoners, Civil Rights, Consumers, Small Farms, Small Business, Free Speech, Democracy; Voting, Religion

The Poor: Education, Health Care, Job and Economic Development, Political Representation, Housing, Food, Clean Water

Prisoners: Education, Counseling, Job Training and Placement, Outside Follow-Up and Support

The Sick: Transportation, Entertainment, Companionship, Home Hospice, Home Service (shopping, pet care, etc.), Access to Treatment, Research, Cures, and Legal Issues

Single Parents: Prenatal Care, Housing, Health Care, Child Care, Job Training

Social Problems: Drug and Alcohol Abuse, Domestic Violence, Youth Violence, Crime, Overpopulation

Teens: Mentoring, After-School Programs, Career Counseling and Job Placement, Programs for "At Risk" Teens, Runaway Counseling and Shelters, Family Planning, Parenting Teens: Skills for Teens with Children, Summer Programs

The Under and Unemployed: Job Training, Language Training, Literacy and GED Programs

Animals

Animal Care: Care and Placement of Strays; Spay and Neutering Programs; Veterinary Services and Vaccines for the Pets of Homebound, Poor or Homeless

Animal Treatment: Greyhounds and Track Horses, Laboratory Animals, the Fur Industry, Meat and Animal Handling

Endangered Species: Whales, Dolphins, Gorillas, Elephants, Rhinos, Tigers, Manatees

Environment
Alternative Energy Sources: Solar, Geothermal, Wind

Destruction of Wildlife and Natural Habitats: Logging, Over-grazing, Rain Forests, Jungles, Lakes, Rivers, Oceans, Reefs, Prairies, Creation of Parks and Reserves

Nuclear Power and Testing

Pollution: Ocean, Air, Ground / Fresh Water, Land, Food, Pesticides, Radioactive Waste, Toxic Waste and Dumping

These are just some of the areas in which you can be of service. If there are others that you have not seen on my list, write them down now:

1 _____

2. _____

3. _____

4. _____

Now, go back over the entire list (including your additions) and *circle ten issues* that are of particular interest to you. Save this list for your charitable contributions.

Of the ten areas you have circled, *put a star next to three* you think you'd really be interested in giving your time to.

How Much of Myself Do I Want to Give?

The next question of course is, "How much time can I give?" That is something only you can determine. Volunteering can mean anything from meeting four times a year for a board meeting, to traveling to a disaster area for six weeks to help local people rebuild, to actually moving to Kazakhstan to teach the staff of local newspapers how to establish and run a free press.

Before you let your guilt kick in, quickly write down how much time you really want to spend on your volunteer work:

_____

This is probably the most honest estimation of how much time you have to give. With so much need in the world, it can be hard to go through your Kaneka and not feel you owe the majority of your new found time to volunteering. But unless you feel strongly about devoting your time to a particular cause, a Wenjen can be just as useful through a combination of charitable giving and part-time volunteering. A cause that seems especially important can simply be given a higher percentage of your annual giving. Sometimes a simple donation can help a charitable or nonprofit organization more than anything else you could do. Think of what would happen if you spent so much time supporting the local theatre that you never got around to writing that Great American Play you know you have in you. We would all be so much poorer for the loss!

If, while reading this, your valiant spirit kicked in and you felt more zealous toward volunteering than accomplishing other items on your other Big List, review your plans again. Then write down a more reasonable time for you to spend volunteering:

_____

The amount of time you allot to your volunteer work is very important, for the next step is to decide exactly how you want to participate in your chosen venture(s). To make time available for your other Big List plans (as well as for your partner's plans), you must have an idea of how much time you want to spend volunteering.

What Can I Do?

What can you do?!?

You are one of the most highly skilled people in your field, with years of experience both inside and outside the workplace. You've spent your life and work developing and honing skills that among other things have brought you quite a sizable income. Certainly any of these skills would be helpful to someone in need. Perhaps you have learned how to manage a business well – what nonprofit doesn't need this insight? Perhaps you are an attorney who enjoys going to court for a good cause – certainly there is a need for you! A psychologist? Doctor? Accountant? What aid organization couldn't use your guidance and assistance?

But just because you used to do a certain job doesn't mean you have to continue it in your volunteer life. An executive in an accounting firm, for example, probably spends more time in management, organization, and administration than in doing mere math. So, just because you were an accountant doesn't mean you have to relegate yourself to doing your church's books if you are really more interested in helping with its youth programs. Or maybe over the years you developed a mean repertoire of jokes. Certainly these abilities would be just as valuable to high school students as your number crunching would be to the church staff.

As a part of your present volunteer work you should look only to those skills and abilities that you especially enjoy and would like to continue doing.

List seven skills, abilities, talents, or tasks that you enjoy:

_____

_____

_____

_____

_____

_____

_____

Now think about how to apply those skills to the three areas you put a star next to on the list. Explore these ideas in your journal.

It is possible that an answer will appear immediately. In my case, I worked with computers, I enjoy fundraising (for a worthy cause), and I am interested in children's education.   So establishing a computer education program in a troubled elementary school seemed right up my alley.   For other people, it could take a little more figuring to see how their skills can fit in.

If "organization, research, and problem solving" came up on your list, you might not immediately see how these skills can help the elderly or teens at risk, but they can! Any board of directors or action group for a nonprofit can benefit from that experience. If you love working with children,   there   are   Head-Start   Programs,   Tutoring   and   Reading Programs, Mentoring, Church Youth Programs, and Area Summer Camp Programs. If you enjoy teaching, you can be a docent at the Zoo or Natural History Museum or Art Museum. You can give history tours of your city.   You can teach in an after-school program, teach evening classes at City College, teach a high school adult program, or teach at the local University in your area of expertise.   Are you a great businessperson and still love every minute of it?   You can be a fundraiser, provide administrative support, or work on an advisory board. Or have you tired of working at a desk and now just want to do something with your hands?   Contact the program run by former

President Jimmy Carter called Habitat for Humanity. It builds homes for people who couldn't afford to buy their own home. Check out building programs locally and abroad, create urban gardens, or even try disaster relief projects. The choice is all yours.

If you still aren't sure how to contribute, investigate the three areas you starred on your list and find out which volunteer groups are actively involved in those areas. The Internet is, as always, a great place to start, and many cities have publications of local charities and not-for-profits as well. Another great way to find a solid group is from personal referrals. Put out feelers for groups that others like you have already found satisfying.

Once you find a group that is doing particularly appealing work in your area of interest, contact it to see where you can fit in. In choosing any volunteer group or project, approach it professionally, just as you did in your career. Get as much information as possible about the organization and the people you would be working with. What would your "job description" and duties be? (If you were a VP making major decisions about many projects, then stuffing envelopes may not get your full attention or it might be a welcome job.) Find out how the organization actually functions. Realize that secretarial and other kinds of support might not be available in volunteerism and that you may have to "make do." Check to see whether there are "emergency meetings," whether you are to be reimbursed for personal expenses, or whether training will be provided. (Before becoming involved with a mentoring program, I had twenty hours of training in working with "kids at risk[1]"). Finally, do not make a commitment until you are certain you want to devote your time to that particular project.

Just "volunteering" probably won't meet your psychological needs. You need to find a position that feels good. Some concepts may sound great at first, but in actuality they can be quite challenging – even frustrating. You should realize that certain volunteer tasks require a great deal of effort and a real time commitment if you expect to be successful at them.

---

[1] "Kids at risk" are children that certain agencies have profiled as coming from an environment that puts them at a higher risk of becoming drug users, gang members, or simply nonproductive members of society.

I mentored a sixth grader named Miguel for five years. When we began, his school was ready to suspend him, he had some major problems at home, and given his situation he seemed ripe for joining a gang. Miguel is now the assistant manager in an electronics store and attends City College. Fortunately, he was able to avoid the pitfalls of gang life and drug usage that surrounded him and become a productive member of society. Mentoring gave him the support he needed to make this successful transition. By being a mentor you can make a huge different in a child's life, and you are making the world a better place, one child at a time. But to do it successfully takes a great deal of time and a long-term commitment. Not every Wenjen is going to be able to offer support in this way. Nor does every one need to.

Another project I volunteered for was bringing food to a homeless shelter and serving the Sunday meal. This activity was satisfying in a completely different way. I knew I was being useful and that the homeless people appreciated it, but because it was done as a group, if I missed one Sunday, someone else could fill in and I didn't feel that the work had gone undone. Working at the homeless shelter didn't have the same level of satisfaction for me as my work with Miguel, but it offered me the flexibility I needed at the time to pursue other activities and still serve. In the end, only you can decide what will successfully fulfill both your desire to utilize your skills in the service of others and your commitment to accomplishing your other Big List goals.

To Work or Not to Work – That Is Not the Question!

Over the years you probably have not had the time to pursue leisure activities as much as you would like. There is nothing wrong with making them more of a priority now. However, few workaholics can retire completely. They get too much satisfaction out of their work. The good news is that as a Wenjen you have the flexibility to work only at your heart's desire and still give as much time as you like to those long-neglected leisure activities. By carefully incorporating your idea of work into your Big List goals, your "Active-Retirement" might actually become one of the most fulfilling and enjoyable working periods of your life. You might even discover the secret behind why some people actually look forward to retirement – it's because they know how to do it right!

Summing Up

Work provides important contributions to our lives. This fact does not change in Active-Retirement. What does change is that income is not a factor for Wenjens. So for those of you who still enjoy your profession or aspects of your profession, I advise the following:

1. Accept the fact that you no longer need to continue to work in the manner you have become accustomed to, as your needs are both changing and will be met by your new Big List plans.

2. There are ways to continue enjoying your former work without continuing the job itself.

3. Consulting, mentoring, or starting one's own business are intensive options that need to be looked at carefully for how they might interfere with other Big List goals.

4. Investing, seeding start-ups, or serving on a board of directors are all strong options that will allow more freedom.

5. Volunteering provides an opportunity to continue utilizing your skills and benefit others. However, make sure you take the time to find a position that realistically suits your skills, time, and desire to be of service.

Liberty is being free from the things we don't like in order to be slaves of the things we do like.
~ Ernest Benn ~

Hobbies are wonderful. You are limited only by your imagination. One can collect, build, fashion, or repair anything. It is all based on individual desire. Many of the Kanekas I interviewed included hobbies – either current, neglected, or desired – on their Big Lists. One of my Big List goals includes building a balsa model airplane. As a child I started many models whenever I was sick in bed, but somehow I never managed to finish any. Someday I will complete one.

Hobbies can be built around anything you derive pleasure from. But unlike activities, which I talk about in other chapters, hobbies seem to revolve around things: making things, repairing things, and collecting things.

Making and Repairing Things: Crafts

Making things is one of the joys of being human. Crafts allow us to create objects of use and beauty and take part in craftsmanship and even artistry without having to be an expert in the field. Woodworking, jewelry making, ceramics, furniture refinishing, sewing, quilting, and model making are just a few of the crafts Kanakas often desire to explore.

Crafts enable us to work with tools and materials and to express our tastes and interests creatively. And they generally do not require extensive training or investment of time to acquire acceptable results. Usually they need only desire, a little know-how, and the proper tools and materials.

For some, one of the most satisfying aspects of craftwork is actually the acquiring and using of the tools and materials required for the task. After years in an office, getting one's hands on a power saw can be invigorating in and of itself! One Kaneka I interviewed had the most wonderful tool collection I had ever seen. He had twenty-seven types of screwdrivers and ninety-two sets of different size screws. He had saws with eight teeth per inch, saws with ten, saws with twelve, and saws with eighteen. His collection filled up a double garage. It took him three years to collect all those tools. As far as I know he hasn't built or repaired anything yet, but he has had a great time collecting.

Collecting

Some people do not collect anything. Others collect everything! Collecting can be insidious. The collector gene seems to make one see potential collections everywhere. To those afflicted, the innate human ability to see somewhat similar objects and say, "These things all belong together!" makes almost any group of two or more things seem like an instant collection. One day I noticed that my wife had two different English teapots. About a month later I noticed there were now three. I "innocently" asked her if she was starting a collection. She confessed she was. However, she was lucky to be able to restrain the collector bug when she realized she didn't actually want a collection of teapots anyway!

It is amazing what people *do* want though. A simple search on the Internet brings dumbfounding results. There are Web sites, on-line stores, and user groups for people collecting Beanie Babies; Pokemon cards; sports memorabilia (cards, photos, clothing, equipment); stamps; coins; foreign currency; comics (books, characters, lunch boxes, costumes); models (cars, trains, rockets, boats, airplanes, helicopters, buildings, historical battlefields); fossils; antiques; dolls (china, horses, period, Kachinas, African, Barbie, GI-Joes, Stars Wars); plants (roses, orchids, Chia-Pets); children's toys (Furbies, Transformers, Legos, Teddy Bears, Tin-Toys, any action figure, matchbox cars, toys given out at fast-food restaurants); dishware; china; cartoon-covered glassware; furniture; movie memorabilia (anything); records (45s, imports, jazz, classical, master recordings); historical artifacts (weapons, uniforms, letters); knives; guns; swords; cameras; Disney (all of it); frogs (the stuffed animals and the flower holders); cow paraphernalia; Jim Beam bottles; statuettes; and art, just to name a few.

My wife, and I have started a variety of collections at one time or another. Often we eventually abandoned them and headed off in another direction. I enjoyed every one though. I can't tell you anything about Pokemon cards, but there are plenty of others I have tried.

Art

My wife and I really enjoy collecting graphic prints. It permits us to collect artists whose paintings we could not afford. We collect prints of both established contemporary artists and old masters. If you desire the real thing, collecting the works of newer artists can be much more affordable; however, it takes real training to know (guess) what will retain its value. Of course there is always the option of simply buying what you like. That should be the point of art anyway, shouldn't it?

Collecting folk art on your travels can also be a lot of fun. Pieces of great beauty and incredible artisanship that would cost a relative fortune back home can often be purchased directly from the artist for a tenth of the sum of retail. You return home with a beautiful object infused with memories of your trip to exotic lands, and in return the artist gets properly reimbursed for his hours of fine handcraftsmanship.

Autographed Books

We have always collected books, and because we are lucky enough to live in a community that appreciates literature, there are always book signings to go to. After we had a few books autographed – we thought we should start a collection! We soon recognized (twenty-three books later) that this passion for signatures wasn't really matching our reading patterns – and that we had run out of shelf room. So, we stopped collecting them. We still collect books, both old and new, but we only keep those we cherish or think we will look at again.[1]

Baseball Cards

If you're a sports fan you could start collecting baseball cards. Or you could just dig up your old collection from the attic. A word of caution though – do not mix collecting with making money. I know the prices for baseball cards have risen dramatically over the years, but I would advise you to collect them for fun. I learned the hard way never to

---

[1]I have a rule that if I haven't looked at a book in thirty years, I can give it away.

mix pleasure activities with money making ones. I tried it and lost both money and the pleasure.[2]

Of course, if you have tired of a collection and want to make space for another (in the attic), then go ahead and sell it. There are collector's shops that can buy entire collections or piece them out on consignment. There are also many trading and selling specialty sites on the Web. And if you want ease, you can always just sell your collection on that wonderful money pit called eBay. I call it that simply because every time I browse it, I buy something. And you have no more discipline than I do. I know, because you purchased this book on a whim.

Books and Letters

There are many ways to go about collecting books. From coffee table books on modern design to various translations of Russian novels, this hobby can be a used- bookstore junkie's dream. One person we know started collecting first edition books and eventually branched out to letters written by historical figures. This seemed like a wonderful way to access both the mind of the writer and a particular moment in history.

Cameras

I love cameras. I think they are beautiful pieces of precision machinery. I've just started a collection that will consist of all the major cameras of my life. Recently I have purchased a WW2 Leica, a Kodak Retina 111C, and am currently on the lookout for a Contax 111 and an Exacta VX. This collection already feels like fun.

One way to enhance the camera collecting experience is to collect photographs taken with each model of camera you have – whether a professional photographer takes them or you take them yourself. Sometimes film stocks and lenses can be hard to find for older cameras, but camera shops that sell and repair older cameras often have connections to individuals who are still manufacturing or repairing these specialty items.

---

[2] I have collected stamps since I was 8 years old. I was the only one in our stamp club that had a catalog and traded two mint American stamps for a cancelled German stamp with a zeppelin on it. It is now worth a lot of money. When there was a frenzy in stamps as an investment I invested and lost a lot of money. It took the fun out of collecting stamps.

Cars

We have a friend who collects Corvettes of all sizes – toys, models, and cars. If you don't happen to have the storage space for ten to twelve cars in your garage, consider the amazing array of model cars available. A progressive collection of models can beautifully exhibit the engineering and design history of a particular make of automobile. You might also enjoy the idea of collecting actual cars. The car you drove in high school is probably heading toward classic status (especially if it was a Dusenburg). Perhaps you could buy one and restore it. The only thing greater than finding a rusted out old Hupmobile in someone's barn is being smart enough to walk away from it and never look back.

Coins

Coins are generally collected by time period, country, or denomination. Personally, I found U.S. coins to be the most interesting. There are some good books as well as monthly magazines that specifically deal with U.S. coins. If one travels a bit, a foreign coin collection can often get started quite inadvertently – though that dusty dish on your dresser full of lira, francs, and dinar (and the occasional New York subway token) probably won't sell for that much on eBay. Along those lines, I don't recommend using coins as an investment, although many dealers will try to sell them to you as such. When I started my collection, I thought coins would be a good hedge against inflation. I was wrong. I sold my collection.

Dolls

This is one of the largest hobbies in the United States. The reason it is so popular is that it can be focused to any personal interest. A collection can be oriented around everything from a favorite TV show to a historical period to a specific area of the world. For a long time I was in love with Santa Fe and the tri-cultural elements that existed in the area. Out of that appreciation came a collection of Pueblo Indian Kachina Dolls. I don't travel to the area as frequently anymore, and I no longer buy Kachinas, but I still love them and think they make a wonderful subject for a collection.

Given the great interest and wide variety of doll collections, there are a few thousand Web sites devoted to doll collecting alone. A Web portal that can lead you to many doll-oriented sites is www.collectingnation.com/help. Also, Hobby House Press (900 Frederick Street, Cumberland, MD, 21502) specializes in books on doll collecting.

Plants (and Gardens)

I mentioned gardening in the exercise section but it is also a wonderful hobby for collecting types of plants, planters, and landscaping styles. My wife now has more than a hundred different types of roses. They are an especially beautiful collection and a joy to behold. Our house is decorated with roses most of the time.

Plant collecting is a wonderful hobby to integrate into your travel plans. I know of a man who collects hot chili peppers. Whenever he goes to a country with especially hot chilies, he researches the plants and imports them. Now he has a many-tiered garden containing most of the hottest chili peppers in the world. His array of homemade salsas are dangerous. If you are looking for new plants to incorporate into your garden, you could visit the many wonderful botanical gardens and parks around the world. Among my favorites are the Burchart Gardens in Vancouver, BC; the Brooklyn Botanical Garden in New York; the Rose Gardens in Portland, Oregon; and Descanso Gardens in Los Angeles.

Pottery

Whenever we travel we visit secondhand stores, collectable stores, antique stores, and swap meets. In the process my wife discovered some pottery from the '40s that she really liked and started collecting it. It has now become very popular.

Pre-Columbian pottery is an area that fascinates me as are artifacts from various other historical periods, though so far I have managed to resist the temptation to start my own pottery collection. We shall see how long that lasts.

Stamps

I started collecting stamps as a young child and still jump in and out of it. Collecting stamps can be a fascinating tool for learning geography, history, and politics, though when I was young there were a lot fewer countries to keep up with (though many of the new countries issue lovely stamps). I have found that the way to liven up a stamp collection is to focus on a particular interest – be it art, sports, or famous writers – and build the collection around that. Perhaps you could tie your collection to books you have read or to a period of art you particularly enjoy. Collecting stamps from countries you have visited is also satisfying – though as you travel more, this method could get out of hand. Regardless of your focus, there are numerous web sites and eGroups where you can find the stamps you want. The U.S. Postal Service also has a good book on stamp collecting. Which makes sense doesn't it?

Wine

Wine collecting is an erudite hobby and can make for many a wonderful meal. (Collecting old beer bottles just doesn't have the same panache. Although, according to reports from the local college, beer bottles are easier to stack into a pyramid in the living room.) Wine collecting also offers a wonderful opportunity for travel. The wine countries of the world are some of the most lovely to visit and tour. Sipping fine wine and eating cheese under a terrace of grapevines isn't such a bad way to spend a Wednesday afternoon, either. Also, when you get back home, your week spent in Napa or Bordeaux will be well remembered when you open that bottle several winters from now. After a glass, I am sure you will feel warm enough to describe to your guests the wonderful trip to buy the bottle as well.

Collections are as personal as one's individual taste. They can be made, abandoned, pursued, displayed and rekindled. They are a wonderful passion that adds a layer of pleasure to a day trip and to travels abroad. In fact, you may have noticed that travel came up in many of the collections that my wife and I have pursued. In your Kaneka transition, collecting and travel often make great bedfellows. An appreciation of trains can be expressed both by a model train collection and by riding train lines worldwide. A baseball card collection can elicit a trip to the Baseball Hall of Fame. Stamps, coins, art, plants, dolls, and many other collections can be made international through your travels. Collecting is a hobby that can be made as flexible and travel-ready as your other Kaneka plans require. The point is simply to be able to enjoy all your passions.

All hobbies are by nature passions. Identifying and pursuing your passions are at the heart of your successful Kaneka transition. So if you find that your woodworking project becomes merely a great tool collection – you have simply identified your collecting gene. Or if you find that your passion for your coin collection has been replaced by a fascination with Kilim rugs after your last trip to the Middle East – so be it! Your Kaneka transition is simply about identifying your passions and pursuing them passionately – whatever they may turn out to be.

Summing Up

Ultimately any hobby can be a worthwhile Kaneka goal. If collecting is your hobby, keep in mind that your focus may change. It is a great reminder that the Big List, although specific, needs to remain flexible about what you want to pursue along your Chen Tao. So in terms of hobbies and collecting, my suggestions are:

1. Identify what hobby or hobbies thrill you and include them on your Big List, no matter how "silly." If it gives you joy it is worth doing.
2. Utilize your hobbies for joy, not for income. Do not confuse collecting with investment.
3. Not every collection needs to be continued. Only collect what presently gives you joy (and give yourself permission to rid yourself of ones that don't any longer).
4. In collecting, allow your other Kaneka goals to influence the discovery of new collections – and vice versa!

*Exercise ferments the humors, casts them into
their proper channels, throws off redundancies
and helps nature in those secret distributions,
without which the body cannot subsist in its
vigor, nor the soul act with cheerfulness.*
~ Joseph Addison ~

*Too many people confine their exercise to jumping to
conclusions, running up bills, stretching the truth, bending over
backward, lying down on the job, sidestepping responsibility
and pushing their luck.*
~ Author Unknown ~

You might have already put a sport or physical activity down on
your Big List. Or you might not have. Either way, we need to discuss
regular exercise (i.e., not just weekend sports or activities), because it is
going to be very hard to achieve any of your Big List goals without it.

Do I Have to?

We already know that regular exercise is necessary for good health
and a long life. It is crucial in maintaining all the body's systems. But
scientists have recently discovered that it affects much more. Unlike
previously thought, the brain *does* continue to grow new brain cells
throughout one's entire life. In fact, it grows them most actively in the
brain centers that are the most crucial for higher thinking. However, and
this is a big however, scientists also found that in older adults these new
brain cells only survive with *regular exercise* (thus giving new meaning
to the term muscle-head)!

Regular exercise isn't something that just extends life either – not
getting it will actually shorten your life. Witness the fact that couch
potatoes are now put in the same insurance category as smokers. (If you
didn't notice a "couch potato" box when you filled out insurance forms,
it is short hand for "exercises less than twenty minutes).

But just because we know the facts about exercise doesn't mean that
we do it. Or that we want to do it. Many of us traditionally had to fight
for enough time just to kiss our spouses and wave to our kids at the end
of a long day. Furthermore, some of us don't feel quite like the youthful

fountains of vim and vigor that we imagine we once were. Exercise might seem like it is just going to be an additional drain of time and energy.

Well, there is good news and there is bad news. The good news is that you now have the time for regular exercise. Even better – that same exercise will put an additional spring in your step that will allow you to accomplish not only everything you *have* to do, but everything you *want* to do as well.

The bad news is that you actually have to do it (but you at least have the means to find ways of making it enjoyable).

So How Do I Start?

First things first, ***Before starting (or upgrading) any exercise program, consult your doctor!*** Maybe you feel fit as a fiddle, but perhaps a little advice on your blood sugar levels before and after exercise, or some insight into what your optimal heart rate is, will prove to be as beneficial as doing the exercise itself. The point is to maintain health – not to jump in blindly, over-exert and feel worse for it! There are constantly new discoveries and improvements in nutrition and physical fitness, and your doctor is one of the experts you should consult with, if not just for safety, but to save you time, frustration, and pain along the road.

So What Do I Do?

Unless they were on your Big List (and your doctor approves), running a four-minute mile, climbing Mount Everest, and tackling the Iron-man Triathlon are not what I am suggesting you achieve. The more frequent the exercise the greater the benefit, but you don't have to overdo it. What is important is to get into shape and stay that way.

But how does one go about getting in shape? Is the only way to "just do it" as the ad suggests? For anyone who has tried exercise programs before and failed, the answer is clearly no.

A personal trainer was asked what the key to a successful exercise program was. His answer – "It must satisfy your head." His point was that we need exercise that stimulates, not exhausts our heads with boredom or frustration. To that end, he suggested that variation was the spice of the exercise life. And not just for the conscious mind alone. The central nervous system actually needs a variety of stimuli to continue to make improvements on the muscular level. Rest is also needed in between workouts. If the nervous system does not have the proper time to recover, there will be no real progress. So the key to getting in shape is variation and regular, but not daily, exercise.

Even if you already have a good exercise program, I suggest you review it and perhaps add a few new sports or activities. This will stimulate muscles unused by your regular routine, give your regularly used muscles a rest, and add the needed stimulus to that most active muscle – the brain. It may also be helpful to have a "second" sport in case some physical problem occurs that stops you from continuing your primary one.

Over the years, I have talked to runners who have pounded their knees to the point of being unable to run, tennis players with rotator cuff injuries who now can't serve, and golf players who have forgotten how to add.

Aerobic Exercise

You know these exercises – they are the ones that make your lungs burn before your thighs do. Aerobic exercise raises your heart rate and thereby strengthens and improves the cardiovascular and metabolic systems of the body (i.e., it strengthens your heart and burns a lot of calories). This is accomplished by any exercise in which the larger muscles (legs, arms) are moved quickly and vigorously. Obviously this will also tone and firm those same muscles in the process. Walking, running, biking, aerobics, tennis, swimming, and kickboxing are all aerobic exercises.

Anaerobic Exercise (Strength Training)

These are the exercises that make you "buff." They focus on strengthening and building muscle tissue. Lifting free weights, using the weight equipment or machines at the gym, and performing strength calisthenics such as push-ups, pull-ups, or sit-ups are all anaerobic exercises. Anaerobic exercise also improves the metabolism as increased muscle mass burns more calories around the clock. Anaerobic exercise is crucial to successful aerobic exercise as it provides the strength needed to perform these exercises properly, thereby getting their full benefits and avoiding injury. It is also very good for women for bone strengthening. Developing proper strength is an important aspect of all exercise. According to a ski-resort physical therapist, most skiing injuries are caused by people whose brain synapses still know how to make their legs ski, but whose leg muscles are just not strong enough to do everything they used to.

Flexing Exercises

These build strength like other types of exercise, but they also move fluid throughout the joints. These fluids act like motor oil does for your engine: they help keep the joints cool, lubricate all the tendons and ligaments, and help prevent injury – to muscles, tendons, ligaments, even bones. Flexing exercises also flush blood, vitamins, minerals, water, and needed nutrients to muscles and joints. Post-workout, flexing a muscle flushes away lactic acid (that stuff that makes your muscles burn during the workout and sore for days afterward) and this allows the muscle to get more of what it actually needs (blood, vitamins, minerals, etc.). Flexing exercises can be done alongside other workouts or as an integral part of the workout itself – such as in yoga, Pilates, modern dance, or ballet.

A successful long-term exercise program is built from a regular variety of all three forms of exercise. To this end, regardless of your other chosen sports and activities, I would strongly suggest
1.   That you join a good health club.
2.   That you hire a personal trainer.

Join a Good Health Club

Regardless of your exercise of choice, you will rarely be able to achieve all three types of exercise, or the variety your brain will require, with one routine alone. Finding a good health club will allow you the flexibility you need to achieve your full physical health, as well as offer you the luxury of support and relaxation.

By a good health club I do not mean the cheapest, the one that's open 24 hours a day, or the one that has the best bodies. I mean the one that is clean, comfortable, charges on a monthly basis (not just annually), and has an abundance of good equipment and personal trainers, a sauna, a steam bath, a pool, and preferably a massage and spa on the premises. The last feature is becoming more common.

Health clubs offer you many benefits. First of all, you can get all three types of exercise at most of them. Also, most offer a variety of exercise classes – from boxing to Pilates to spinning – so that no mind should ever become bored. Feasibly, your workouts could vary every time you went to the gym. Let's say your three workouts for the week included an aerobics class, an hour of weight training with a trainer, and a yoga class. Or you could mix it up every time you went by riding the stationary bike for twenty minutes (while watching CNN), doing strength training for another twenty minutes, and then taking a twenty-minute flex class. Whatever pleases you the most that week, as long as you are getting all three types of exercise.

Another benefit of health clubs is that they give you access to the newest and best exercise equipment (i.e., not the stuff advertised on television late at night). This equipment is designed specifically for individual body needs. For example, there are new non-impact machines that help save the knees (such as the elliptical trainer, which is a great replacement for the treadmill). Health club equipment is also generally geared for strengthening specific areas of your body. This can be very helpful in all aspects of your physical life. For instance, if you suffer from lower back problems (a very common ailment), there are specific machines that can help you build up muscles to support that area and alleviate some of the pain.

The amount of time spent going to the club will depend on the type of program that best suits you. Some people find it easier to go for a one-hour workout, twice a week, with some tennis, golf, or other sport on the weekends. Others find it easier to work out for just twenty minutes, five times a week, with a small walk in the mornings. It doesn't matter how you mix it up as long as you are working out *at least* twenty minutes, three times a week. My advice would be to work up a weekly program with your trainer.

Hire a Personal Trainer

I recommend using a personal trainer at least once a week to help you focus and to design your workout. Give your trainer your goals, your preferences (I hate sit-ups, I only want to have to do this twice a week, I love jazzercise), and your doctor's recommendations. If you need to lose some weight in the process, ask your trainer about diet as well (and go over any recommendations he or she gives you with your doctor). Then let your trainer design a program for the week that fits your needs, altering it as often as the trainer sees fit. Some people like to work out with a trainer every time they go to the gym. If that is what you want, find a trainer (usually at or referred by your health club or a friend at the club) whose method works best for you. It is all about what works best for you. Working with a trainer is like seeing a shrink (but much cheaper): they direct you, keep track of your progress, and listen to your stories. And working out with a trainer can really help pass the time. It is also a hundred times better than working out with a friend (or your partner) because your trainer will never try to convince you to skip the workout and catch a matinee.

Variety Is the Spice of the Active Life!

So what are your options? Obviously, if you are retiring from the circus, unicycle riding and milk bottle balancing might be your longtime sports of choice. The following sections describe some of the more popular exercises and their benefits. Some of you might choose one as your main form of exercise, while others might work out mainly at the club and vary your sports only on the weekends. Whatever works. Remember – the most important condition of any exercise program is that you enjoy doing it and stick with it.

Bicycling

Mildly to Highly Aerobic, Mildly to Medium Anaerobic

A great sport for people over 50! It also is a wonderful way to explore the countryside. Driving is too fast to really take in a region, and walking is too slow to cover much ground. On a bike you can travel on quiet scenic routes through small towns and villages while enjoying nature (and unlike driving, you can go slow enough to really look at that covered bridge without the risk of accidentally driving into the river). Biking is non-impact and it lets you go at your own pace. Furthermore, you don't need to necessarily leave town to find a nice place to bike: many cities now have bike paths that let you avoid traffic or take you through the more picturesque parts of town.

There are different types of bicycles, and which one you buy can make a marked difference in your biking experience. I would recommend going to a bike store (not a department store) and buying "hybrid" with plenty of gears. I am talking about a bike with medium road tires, a comfortable seat, and handle bars that allow you to sit upright instead of leaning over (which can be hard on the hands, shoulders, and neck). However, it is crucial to get one with at least fifteen gears (more if you can find it), as this is the only way to manage hills. Also be sure to get yourself a good helmet and gloves for safety. Buy a good bike rack for your car so that you can just throw your bike on the back of the car and go cycling somewhere beautiful and traffic-free whenever you please.

There are a number of travel outfits that put together bike trips both here and abroad. Some better known ones are Crossroads, Elderhostel, Bike Vermont, and Butterfield & Robinson. They will usually supply not only guides and lodging but also all the necessary equipment. These companies can help you choose a non-local bike trip that will be a wonderful combination of travel and exercise.

Couples Dancing

Mildly to Highly Aerobic

Folk dancing is great fun and great exercise. The music is lovely and you can adjust your level of cardio-activity by how high you jump or how hard you stomp. Because it's an activity enjoyed by all ages, it gives you the opportunity to do it with the kids and grandkids. Ballroom dancing is generally not as robust, unless you plan to delve into some of the Spanish rhythms, such as tango, salsa, or flamenco. Swing dancing has become very popular recently and there are plenty of venues at which to dance. For the more adventurous among you, Dirty Dancing, a la Patrick Swayze, will certainly get your blood flowing.

Cross-Country Skiing and Snow-shoeing

Highly Aerobic, Mildly to Medium Anaerobic

Cross-country skiing offers a combination of challenging aerobic exercise and beautiful winter scenery. For this reason, it has become an increasingly popular sport, and many downhill resorts have cross-country trails as well. It is a wondrous experience to get out into the wilderness after a new snowfall.

If cross-country skiing seems like too much of a challenge, snowshoeing also offers access to this beautiful scenery. And don't worry – with the new designs in snowshoes, walking is much easier (no more bowlegs) and much more enjoyable.

Dance

Medium to Highly Aerobic, Mildly to Highly Anaerobic, Mildly to Highly Flexing

Dancing is one of the few exercises that occasionally can do it all. That's why you don't see many ballerinas running the track. Although ballet and modern dance encompass all three types of exercise, there are many more options out there – Jazz, African, Interpretive, Caribbean, South American, Native American, Hula – you name it. Universities, community colleges, and adult learning programs are great resources for finding these other dance forms, though many traditional dance studios are now offering alternative forms of dance as well. If you already enjoy dance, a new form is worth a try. A Sunday afternoon learning an African traditional dance to a backup group of drummers can be quite invigorating!

Day Hiking

Mildly to Highly Aerobic

A wonderful sport! A perfect way to experience nature and exercise at the same time. Choose an especially beautiful location and you might not even notice that you are exercising. Hike through the desert of

Joshua Tree National Forest, along the coast of Oregon or through the White Mountains of New Hampshire. The State or National Park Service as well as the Forest Service will have maps of wonderful day hikes. You can call the park service directly (or stop by the ranger station), but maps are often posted or available to take in hand at the head of many trails. Maps of National Parks are also available to download or order online at www.nps.org.

Day hikes come in many different distances and levels of difficulty, so make sure you know your trail before you begin. A great resource for this is your local travel bookstore. There you can find hiking books for local, regional, national, and even international day hiking. Books will generally have maps and detailed descriptions of the views and skill levels of each trail. Purchase a book about hiking in the local region and discover a new and beautiful aspect of your own area each weekend. Knowing that there is more to your area than initially meets the eye will certainly make that in-town traffic seem more bearable midweek. I used to be hesitant about buying a book for $18.95 on hiking in a certain national park I had traveled to. Finally I realized that if I was planning to spend a thousand dollars on my next vacation there, the pleasure of finding a new hiking trail in that area would be worth a more than $18.95.

Downhill Skiing

Mildly to Medium Aerobic, Mildly to Medium Anaerobic

I have been skiing for over fifty years and have loved every minute of it. I currently belong to a group called "The Over the Hill Gang," made up of skiers over age 50.

A number of the members didn't even take up skiing until later in life and have gone on to become quite strong skiers. Outside of individual circumstances, there isn't any reason that one of Kaneka[1] age can't participate in this vigorous sport. I take two to three trips with the Gang every year (my wife skis only occasionally because she has had arthroscopic surgery on both knees). With a good pair of skis (many resorts now rent quite decent equipment), warm dry clothing, and a good

---

[1] "Kaneka": a rebirth into Active-Retirement (traditionally taking place at age 60).

private lesson, one can usually be enjoying this thrilling sport in a day. With it comes a wonderful combination of good company, good exercise, and beautiful scenery.

Gardening

Mildly Anaerobic

Gardening can be great exercise. You get the cumulative effect of carrying, bending, and digging for a total body workout. And if you make your partner help carry all those fifty-pound bags of fertilizer and topsoil, the bags become strength training for the both of you. Gardening also has a wonderful spiritual and inspirational quality. It is constantly fulfilling to plant a seed or seedling and have it grow into a magnificent flower or majestic tree. Gardeners are a class of people who truly see what Aristotle meant when he said that the potential of the flower is in the seed.

Golf

Mildly Aerobic, Mildly Flexing

The exercise benefit of golf is the taking of a three- to four-mile walk over the 18-hole course (no, miniature golf doesn't count). It also builds strength and flexibility in the arms, shoulders, legs, hips, and back. But fundamentally, it is a social game of skill. Golf is a wonderful opportunity to establish new relationships and strengthen old ones. Golfer's stories about "birdies" and "almost a hole in one" are second only to "the bass that got away" stories of fishermen. On the other hand, it was Mark Twain who said, "Golf is a good walk spoiled."

Hiking and "Trekking"

Mildly to Highly Aerobic

For those who like to travel, there are longer-term hikes that can incorporate both the joys of exercise with the joys of new terrain. Be it backpacking through a state wilderness area or strolling through the tulip country of Holland, longer-term hiking can be a glorious experience. There is truly no other way to experience nature as well.

Information regarding self-led backpacking hikes and wilderness areas in the United States can be obtained from the same sources you would use for researching day hiking. The Sierra Club is another resource for good hikes and hiking groups.

The abundance of people who enjoy this particular mode of exercise travel has also created a successful industry of high-level, exotic, and well-led hikes in all parts of the world and for almost every taste. Whether you are looking for a scientific hike through the Galapagos Islands or a wine country hiking tour of Bordeaux, hikes are available in abundance and being led by experts. They can be as extreme as one would expect from the word "trekking," or as luxurious as the day hikes that end at some of the loveliest villas and hotels in the land. The choice is really yours. Some of the top companies in this new field are Country Walkers, Butterfield & Robinson, Abercrombie & Kent, and Geographic Expeditions.[2]

Home Gym

Medium to Highly Anaerobic

A home gym is wonderful but generally should not be looked at as a replacement for the health club.

In most cases it can be great for days when you can't get to the gym or for slipping in an additional workout between times. However, if you are one of those people who feel so put off by working out in a public gym that you avoid working out entirely, by all means, get a home gym

---

info@butterfield.com,   1-800-678-1147).   Abercrombie   &   Kent (www.aandktours.com/html/index.html,   1-800-757-5884).   Geographic Expeditions (www.geoex.com, info@geoex.com, 1-800-777-8183).

right away and just hire a trainer to come to your home. But don't just buy the cheapest apparatus or latest fad you saw on television. You probably won't end up looking like Chuck Norris or Suzanne Somers anyway.

Instead, discuss with your trainer what exercises you should try to include in your workouts and what equipment would best achieve them. Then go to an exercise equipment retailer and purchase a proper piece (or pieces) of equipment to accomplish those exercises (your trainer might actually come with you). Most professional equipment should offer you versatility in your exercise. Make sure you find one that does. If a machine gives you only one way of strengthening your biceps, it will not be giving you the variation you will need. Yes, buying professional-level equipment might cost you more money up front, but it will save you money in the end – because it means you might actually use the thing after you bring it home. Among other things, it is designed to help you avoid injury – and you will certainly be using your equipment more if you remain **able** to keep using it.

Kayaking, Canoeing, and Rowing

Mildly to Medium Anaerobic

Now by kayaking I do not mean the kind where you roll your kayak (and yourself) down rapid whitewater over and between massive rocks. I mean the paddling on the ocean, in a lagoon, or around the lake kind of kayaking. The kind where you are not at risk but are still very close to nature. Often you can see birds, otters, seals, or even whales. And all the while you are getting a wonderful workout for your upper body. This has become such a popular sport recently that several companies are now leading tours that combine kayaking with travel. Butterfield & Robinson[3] offers kayaking trips with themes such as "Tatshsenshini: An Ice Age Journey," "Babine-Skeena: River of the Grizzlies," and "Johnstone Strait: Sea-Kayaking with the Orcas."

In many ways, canoeing can be similar to kayaking. You get the same wonderful gliding feeling as you view river or lake wildlife. However, a word to the wise – I have tipped a canoe, while I have always felt quite stable in a kayak.

---

[3] www.butterfield.com, info@butterfield.com, 1-800-678-1147.

Rowing on a rowing skiff is also a beautiful experience – and adds quite a bit of aerobic exercise by adding leg movement. However skiff-type rowing is so exercise intensive that much of the nature you are rowing through can be lost in the endeavor. I find rowing in a rowboat clumsy, but you certainly won't go fast enough to miss anything.

Running

Highly Aerobic, Mildly to Medium Anaerobic

Running is a very popular sport. Those who are addicted to it are just that – addicted to it! They say it brings them to a different state of mind they can't imagine living without. Many runners also like to add a bit of challenge to their daily routine with 5Ks, 10Ks, and marathons. For most, their race is more against an "inner" competitor than an outer one. Many runners find that this inward focus adds the mental stimulus they need in a sport.

If you have not been a runner up to this point, beginning this sport can be challenging. I would highly suggest that you try walking before you run. It is an idea that is not as clichéd as it sounds. Building up the necessary aerobic and anaerobic strength gradually through walking can make the difference between your trying running just once and your perhaps discovering a sport that you really enjoy. Just be sure that regardless of your present state of conditioning, you always warm up with a brisk walk first, and that you have new running shoes (you need the padding) that are the proper type for your kind of foot and step (yes, they make those these days). Then choose to run on softer surfaces, such as a track or dirt path. I know too many people who have knee problems from years of running, and none of us get very far without our knees.

Swimming

Medium to Highly Aerobic, Mildly to Medium Anaerobic

Doctors seem to always agree on this: swimming is one of the best exercises you can do. Highly aerobic but completely non-impact, the effect of slipping through the water can also be highly soothing for the mind. Whether you are attracted to the meditative repetition of lap upon lap of the freestyle stroke or you enjoy varying your strokes as you swim across a clear lake – the important thing, as with any form of exercise, is to keep moving for at least twenty minutes. Which with swimming isn't too hard since if you stop moving, you will drown.

Water exercise classes, which many health clubs now have, are also becoming a popular alternative to swimming laps. The exercises emphasize both the strength and aerobic benefits of swimming without some of the tedium people experience in the lap pool. In either case, exercise in the water offers an additional buoyancy to the entire frame that is especially helpful for people with prior injuries, as it gives support to the joint and skeletal system during the exercise.

Tennis

Medium to Highly Aerobic, Mildly to Medium Anaerobic

Not only does tennis build hand-eye coordination, speed, and agility it also strengthens the legs and upper body (but make sure to stretch out first). In addition, with "old" tennis players like Steffi Graph (31) still winning matches, you too may have a chance! Over four million of the nation's tennis players are over 50. If you aren't a rabid tennis player, I recommend playing doubles – it allows you to enjoy tennis but without the overexertion.

Walking

Mildly to Medium Aerobic

Good for both the lower and upper body. Also good for the mind! In today's world of heightened activity and constant stimuli, one's mind is constantly on the alert. Walking, with its gentle rhythmic motion, can put one in an altered state where the mind is clear. It is the perfect time to pursue your fantasies or plan your next novel. But by walking, I do not mean a leisurely stroll! A walk for exercise should be at a brisk pace with plenty of arm movement to raise heart levels and increase breathing. And include a few hills for real benefits! Also, take the time to buy a proper pair of walking shoes. Although walking is low impact, the feet still need good support, especially over the long term.

And the Results Are In!

As a person undergoing a Kaneka, you are transitioning into one of the most active and enjoyable periods of your life. If you've always been physically active, you already know how much energy and joy regular exercise brings, and you must have planned for it in your new Chen-

Tao.[4] But if you haven't been keeping in shape and need a little more coaxing to make the space for it, I want to reassure you that the benefits of regular exercise are instantaneous. I am not saying that all the extra weight will be gone tomorrow (though it will soon be on its way). Or that all the aches and pains will instantly disappear (though they are definitely now on their way out). But rather that your head will be clearer, your heart will feel more at peace, and your energy level will be higher (as long as you didn't over-exert) the moment you complete your first good exercise session. And if anything represents the type of life you are creating for yourself on your new Chen-Tao – this is it. It is a life chosen by you to give you joy and create a sense of health and fulfillment. So yes, go out and "just do it" – just do it in a way that you enjoy, because you can!

Summing Up

1. Make the time for regular exercise, because it will supply the vim and vigor you'll need to complete all your fabulous Big List goals.
2. Accept the fact that the time you spend on regular exercise is actually going to give you *more* time and energy in the long run.
3. Consult with your doctor regarding starting or upgrading your current exercise program.
4. Join a good health club (and use it)!
5. Hire a personal trainer to encourage you and design your workouts for you.
6. Variation is the key to a good exercise program. If you don't have more than one sport, start considering a few more.

---

[4] "Chen-Tao": The right life path for you.

When I was young I thought that money was the most important
thing in life;
now that I am old I know that it is.
~ Oscar Wilde ~

Today's financial world can be quite complex. With federal tax, state tax, estate tax, sales tax, syntax, and a multitude of investment vehicles to choose from, financial planning and control are not for the faint of heart or dizzy of head. As a result, there are plenty of qualified (and not so qualified) people who can invest or manage your money for you. There are also many good books and some bad ones on financial planning and investment if you choose to do it yourself. Therefore, it is not my goal to be another person who advises you on how and where to invest your money, or to guide you through the maze of estate planning. In this chapter, I simply want to ask you to look at your basic philosophy of investing and asset control and to make sure that it will fit your new life as a Wenjen.[1]

As an affluent person, you have probably made many investments over the years. Different people handle such accounting in different ways. For some the management of their money is a sport they aggressively play with gusto. Others approach it as a drain of time and energy that they would rather hand over to an "expert." In either case or in any of the cases in between the key to successful money management remains the same: identifying the end goal of the investment.

Up until now the end goal of your investing has probably been to create a sizable nest egg. Or portfolio. Or net worth. Whatever you want to call it, the type of investment you did was geared toward the laying away of an ever-growing amount of wealth – whether it was accessible or not. However now, with the perhaps initially unsettling realization that you will not be sitting up on that perch for eternity, and with your new Big List in hand, a new direction for your investing should begin to emerge.

---

[1] "Wenjen": the affluent person who is enlightened enough to spend his or her time pursuing a "cultured" life.

Making a Plan That Works

In Chapter 4 we discussed a different way of looking at your future finances. First you addressed your and your family's future by coming up with a financial plan that would cover any emergencies or needs for medical and long-term care. You then took this idea a step further by determining the amount of money you wanted to gift to your family, friends and charity in this life. Then you determined the amount that you wanted them to inherit after you are gone. With those concerns out of the way, and with the ultimately freeing acceptance of your eventual perchlessness, you then began to look at your remaining assets as something that could actually be used over this finite period we call life.

Your funds don't need to last forever. And your foresight and planning means that everyone is going to be taken care of. The exciting part is that your affluence leaves you with a healthy amount of money with which to accomplish all those nifty Big List goals!

But your money will still need to be managed. And now it needs to be managed in a fashion that responds to the needs of your new goals. Your old financial strategy was successful (or else you wouldn't be affluent), but now you need a new strategy that will meet the requirements of your new Chen-Tao.[2]

Most financial planners and advisors have their own personal philosophies about investing. In part, that is what you are paying for when you go to them for advice. However, you are choosing a unique path in life, and most of these philosophies will not match up with your goals. Financial planners and advisors generally make plans for people who are following a very different path: the path of acquiring affluence (the path that you used to be on). You, however, have already achieved that goal and now have a new path to pursue: the path of acquiring the freedom to live out your dreams – the path of the Wenjen.

When my wife and I were looking for a financial planner, we wanted someone who shared our investment philosophy. We had two portfolios, a regular and a retirement 401k. Based on our preferences and our Big List plans, we had come up with four investment guidelines:

[2] "Chen-Tao": The right life path for you.

1. Our portfolios were to be diversified throughout products in which we believed. We might not have been exceptionally diversified throughout both our portfolios, but we felt comfortable with our level of diversification.
2. Our other monies were to sit in high-risk assets because we don't necessarily mind losing some money. We know that when you take a risk, certain things are bound not to work out. Of course, we hope more will turn out well than won't, but we are not so unreasonable as to expect a perfect record.
3. We don't mind spending principal, which means we don't have to live on interest or dividends alone.
4. We believe that it is counterproductive to leave one's children (and grandchildren) too much money.

We went out with that philosophy in hand, and yet not one financial planner we talked to had a plan that suited our guidelines. I had to personally modify every plan that was presented to us. You might be luckier than we were and find a financial planner or advisor who can satisfy your needs perfectly. But if not, you may have to do what we did – take their general guidance but hold fast to your own philosophy and mix in a few good ideas of your own.

Unsure of what ideas might meet your future Wenjen needs? Well, I can share with you an overview of a financial plan that might work well for someone on this Chen-Tao. With your financial advisor's input, I am sure you can take it from there.

I believe in dividing assets into three categories:

Base money This is the amount of money that I want to keep intact as principal. I want to draw income from this money. Personally, I would suggest looking for mutual funds with long track records. Don't be drawn in by the superstar of the year. Look for funds with a consistent 15 percent return. Then be sure to find out whether the current manager has been responsible for managing that fund for at least a number of years.

The amount put in the Base Position should vary according to and with your assets. At one to three million dollars in total assets, I would suggest putting about 50% of your assets into this position. Above three million, the percentage could start to drop.

Loose money This is money you can invest a little more aggressively, either in stocks with the help of a financial advisor known for his or her aggressive investment style, or perhaps in real estate. I have found limited partnerships to be the easiest way to invest in real estate. Again, make sure to investigate the track record of the developer – and find out what fees the partnership charges, as many try to take exorbitant fees up front. If your total assets are in the one to three million dollar range, my recommendation would be to put about 25% into Loose Money. Above three million, you can increase this percentage.

High-risk money This is "gambling" money. Recently there has money made (and lost) in Tech and Internet stocks and mutual funds. I have really enjoyed my activities in this area, and you might find you do as well. While I am not recommending any "get rich quick" schemes, it is feasible to get a 25 to 35 percent return on some of the better stocks or mutual funds. Of course, this market depends a lot on what happens in the Internet world. Even so, the entire face of business is rapidly changing and plenty of new businesses will become just as successful in their turn. If your total assets are in the one to three million dollar range, my recommendation would be to put about 25 percent into High Risk areas. Above three million, you can increase this percentage if you feel like it.

This outline, although just a suggestion, is responsive to a Wenjen's future needs and financial plans. First, it creates a constant income through principal that will cover your future needs, any potential emergency, and any gifts and/or inheritance you plan to give to your family. Then it takes the remaining money and puts it to work. This way everyone is taken care of and everyone stands to benefit from the gains of more aggressive investing. In Chapter 5, you accepted that you are not going to be on that perch forever, and in doing so realized that you no longer have to financially plan for immortality. As a result, you have taken the necessary steps to ensure your family's financial security in this life (and beyond). Therefore, regardless of fluctuations in the market or temporary setbacks, you stand only to gain by this more aggressive approach to asset management.

Simplifying Your Financial Situation

Once you have come up with a successful Wenjen financial plan, decide how much time you personally want to spend on your finances. The time needed can vary widely – from annual meetings with a good financial planner who takes care of your investments for you; to quarterly maintenance if you manage your own investments in mutual funds, real estate, and proven stocks; to fairly often if you invest in some of the more volatile stocks. With this in mind, I strongly suggest that you do not become (or stay!) the type of investor who watches his or her stocks three times a day – unless, that is, you really can't find any other interest in life. Yes, I admit, stock watching can be fun, but it probably isn't what you wanted to do when you grew up. Or as much fun as the racecar driving school you put down as Item 2 on your Big List.

The goal then is to simplify your financial management so that you are free to actually go out and enjoy the fruits of your years of labor. To do this, my first suggestion would be to find a good financial planner.

Financial Planners

It seems like everyone is calling himself a financial planner these days. Stockbrokers, lawyers, accountants, and even insurance brokers will all tell you that they are financial planners. Then they will try to sell you their product. A professional financial planner is a different animal altogether and can be very useful. A professional financial planner is a CFP – someone who has taken an exam to get a C(ertified) F(inancial) P(lanning) certificate. CFPs do specialize and can be used for different goals. Whomever you choose, don't use your accountant, lawyer, or insurance agent as a financial planner, as it is not their proper function or purpose.

Financial planners and advisors who sell There are some CFPs who are interested in selling you something – either insurance, certain mutual funds, or Florida swampland. Simply avoid this group all together.

Financial planners and advisors who manage your portfolio
Some CFPs will manage your portfolio for you. For this service they charge a percentage of the portfolio. If you find yourself becoming overwhelmed with a dull, heavy feeling at the thought of managing your own portfolio, this may be the way to go. But make sure you check up on your financial planner's track record, the type of investments he uses, what his reporting procedures are, and what has been his biggest draw down (loss) on a portfolio.

If you find a CFP who performs to your satisfaction, talk to him/her about your investment philosophy. If you find that he/she keeps coming back to his/hers ideas of investing, without having taken your concepts into account, he/she is not the right person for you. After all, being able to strike out as a Wenjen is a unique privilege that is beyond the reach of many people. As a result, financial plans that are good for "most" people are not necessarily the good for Wenjens. But if you do find a CFP who is willing to use his/hers approach to investing as a way to achieve your stated financial goals, give him/her 20 to 50 percent of your portfolio (a good CFP will probably not work with a portfolio of less than $250,000) for a year and see how he/she does. With all that good planning and research up front, you should feel fairly safe spending all your time writing your novel on the beaches of Tahiti, if that is what you would rather be doing.

Financial advice for a fee Some CFPs offer you the choice of having them manage your portfolio or, for a fee, giving you financial advice so that you can effectively manage it. This can give you some flexibility for when you're in Tahiti next year and need someone to manage your portfolio.

In general, you can expect to pay a high hourly rate for this type of advice – but in my experience it is well worth it. I currently pay my financial advisor $350 an hour. I spend about three hours with her every quarter, during which we discuss the plan for the following quarter. I also contact her if there is a major change in the market.

Do the research Before engaging any CFP, you should check out him or her (thoroughly). Ask them about their background, their education, and whether they have any special investment strategies.

Make sure you get all the information you need to feel comfortable. After all, they will be playing with your money. Also ask them for three references to clients whose situation and philosophies are similar to yours. Comparing yourself with someone who has different ideas about money can be very misleading. A CFP may have created a proven strategy of real-timing, or diversification of bonds, or mutual funds, or "Blue Chip" stocks, but it may not fit into your investment philosophy as a Wenjen.

Regardless of your preference, I am sure that with careful research you can find a CFP and a financial program that will suit your new Wenjen needs. But use a CFP to do it. The point to this entire exercise is to gain time and freedom – and that includes the freedom from having to spend your precious time micro-managing your finances.

Banking

My second suggestion would be to simplify your day-to-day accounting. With today's technologies this process can easily be made quicker, more efficient, and more travel friendly. I suggest trying one of the following ways to simplify banking.

Use your computer Pay your bills online. If you use the Quicken credit card you can also download your statement. Numerous computer programs exist to manage your finances, and many Web sites enable you to pay your bills and do your banking online

I use Wells Fargo Online to manage my accounts and the computer program Quicken to manage my immediate finances. The process is extremely fast and easy. Through Wells Fargo Online, I set up my account so that the bank pays all of my monthly bills automatically. Once the bank receives the amount from the vendor, it simply sends out a bank check and records it in my account. At the end of the month I get copies of the checks and a statement. From there, reconciling my accounts takes only a few minutes. Quicken then allows me to pay any remaining bills with incredible ease, for once I enter the address of any payee, it remembers that address and brings it up automatically when it issues checks or records. Then it issues and prints checks directly from the computer and reconciles the amounts for me. It also allows for writing manual checks, which are easily mixed in with any computer checks and accounted for in the financial reconciliation. And it also allows to download credit card information.

Use your phone Many banks offer pay-by-phone options that have similar features to online services. You can check your balance, deposits, and debits; track checks; and even pay bills. These bills can be scheduled monthly, or amounts and check issue dates can be punched in through the telephone keypad. Again, the bank will send out a check for you and record it on your monthly statement.

Get free mileage Use your credit card. Just charge all your expenses to one credit card. Write one check to the credit card company and the reconciling of your account becomes almost a non-issue. Build up those airline miles and trade them in for travel upgrades (see Chapter 8 on Travel). There are a number of reasonable credit cards with fixed annual percentage rates in the 8 to 12 percent range that have no annual fee. However, since the main reason for having a credit card is to get mileage, this shouldn't be that much of a concern as you should be paying off your debt every month.

Hire a firm to handle your bills or get a personal assistant This, unfortunately, can still require a great deal of input from you, at least up front. Any changes to your situation can require another considerable outlay of time and information. You will also find that in order for any outside person or firm to be effective, you will have to be very consistent in both your spending methods and record keeping. You will also have to make sure that records of each and every expenditure you make are recorded intelligibly (not in your private short-hand) and made available to the person(s) handling your accounts in a timely fashion.

Even with these (perhaps large) adjustments, it still can be a tremendous relief to not think about one's day-to-day financial affairs for stretches at a time. After all, who wants to worry about when the gas bill is due when you're in the middle of climbing Everest?   That peace of mind alone can make it worth all the effort you had to expend in your "down" time.

Protect and Guide It

Now that you have gone to all the trouble of setting up systems to manage your money, you had best take measures to protect it and ensure that it is used according to your wishes long into the future.

Get a Lawyer

Surprisingly, many of the Kaneka-ing3 people I interviewed did not have a personal lawyer. There is no good reason for any affluent person to go through today's complicated legal world without the benefit of an attorney.

Don't get me wrong. I hate lawyers, even though some of them are my best friends. But in a world of irrevocable trusts, wills, living wills, estate planning, gifting, charitable remainder trusts, powers of attorney for healthcare, and litigious people everywhere – you must have a lawyer. Therefore, it is best to have one who knows you and the specifics of your situation. So choose an attorney according to your main legal needs and think of the attorney as you would your primary physician – if your primary attorney thinks you need a specialist (tax, estate, etc.), he or she can always refer you to another qualified attorney. This way there is always one person who always knows your entire history and circumstances and is overseeing your general legal "health" care.

The Legal List

There are several basic documents that I would have you draw up as legal preparation for your life as a Wenjen. As all areas of your life are undergoing a transformation during your Kaneka, your legal needs are no exception.

This Legal List, as opposed to the "Big List," is a group of documents you should either have or at least be aware of in case at some point you need them.

Living trust A legal "mirror maze" that lets you control your assets by essentially storing them in a "box." Rather than your accumulated assets being considered in their individual parts (your house, bank

---

3 "Kaneka": a rebirth into Active-Retirement

accounts, etc.), your assets are held in a "trust." This trust can then pass as a single asset to a named beneficiary when you finally fall off the perch.

Let me give you an example from my own life of how living trusts can benefit their beneficiaries – and how the absence of living trusts can make for endless headaches. When my mother refinanced her house, her bank took the property out of her living trust and did not return it. When she died and left me the property, I tried to sell it – and had to go through endless legal loops (probate), spend a considerable amount of money on attorneys, and ended up having to wait a year before I could complete the transaction. None of this would have been necessary had the property been returned to the trust in the first place.

Given my experience, constructing a living trust is a must for a Kaneka who is planning for his or her family's future. Ask your attorney for a broader explanation of the implications of a living trust to its beneficiaries. However, outside any additional advice your lawyer should give you, my basic rules for living trusts are:

1. Create a living trust.
2. Move all your assets into it.

Living wills This is a formal document that expresses an individual's desire for the amount and extent of medical care that should be administered to him/her in case of terminal illness or injury. This process should be your decision, not that of your doctor or your relatives. This is something to be considered seriously in light of your religious or other beliefs. Do not place the burden of the decision on your partner or children. In the event that you are terminally ill or injured, what your family will need most is one another's support, not the option of being torn apart by conflicting opinions over the best way to manage your situation. For this reason above all others, living wills are a necessary way of ensuring your family's future as a happy family long after you are gone.

Wills Creating a living trust does not remove the need for a will. You are in control of your life, so you should also be in control of who inherits your assets. Still, two out of three Americans die without one. But you have one, right?

Once you have created a will don't let it become a dead document.4 A will should be reviewed every three years as your family and financial situations change (and I trust you won't use it as a threat to your children in order to get your way – "If you don't eat your broccoli I will cut you out of my will!") There are also periodic changes in estate tax laws that will require a will to be reviewed and potentially amended.

Let me also make a few observations that might help you avoid some post-fall-off-the-perch family squabbles. Some of the biggest rifts in families are created by the "reading of the will" and the distribution of assets. As I have repeatedly mentioned, I am a strong believer in giving while you are still alive. The pleasure of that act cannot be overstated. However an added benefit of gifting in life is that this gifting does not have to be made in equal proportions to all of your children. There may be a greater need in one family, or another family may have more children to educate (your grandchildren) or may need extra support to start a business. Responding to a given need with variable gifting during life can be done gracefully. However, I strongly suggest that in your will you leave equal amounts to all your children, regardless of need. I know this may not make sense to you as parent, but showing favoritism from the grave can cause a major problem, whereas equal giving after death will avoid a major conflict (that you will not be around to rectify or smooth out).5

My next suggestion is that you specify to whom any jewelry, art, antiques, or other items of individual or sentimental value are to go. We've let the kids look at all our art and decide which pieces they want. Their choices have been specified in a codicil to our will. Just remember that although a will is designed to fulfill your wishes when you are gone, the distribution of your assets will probably serve everyone better if it is done with minimum of disagreement among your children in your absence.

---

[4] Pun intended.

[5] I would make an exception for a child or family where there is an expensive medical problem. However, I would still give everyone an equal amount but allocate an additional amount for special purpose.

Re-marriage and nuptial agreements There is one more item I would like to touch on. In the event you and your spouse separate due to death or divorce, and you eventually decide to get remarried, you should create both a prenuptial and a postnuptial agreement. Though many respond to the initial idea of these agreements with distaste, this type of agreement protects both partners and avoids many future arguments within the greater family. These agreements are especially important if there are children, and made even more so if the financial resources of one partner is far more extensive than those of the other. This way, should you pass away first, you can provide for your new partner's needs while still ensuring that your children (or your new spouse's children) do not feel that your partner or partner's family has in some way "stolen" their inheritance from them.

Summing Up

Since you are changing your life path to that of a Wenjen, it is time for you to make sure your financial plans reflect that change. To this end, I suggest the following:

1. Understand that you have unique financial goals as a Wenjen (as explored in this chapter and as further discussed in Chapter 5).
2. Research and find a qualified CFP who is willing to work with your unique financial philosophy.
3. Simplify your day-to-day financial accounting.
4. Get a primary lawyer.
5. Draw up all the proper legal documentation to protect your assets and their eventual distribution.
6. These things having been accomplished, you will then be remarkably free to get on with the more important things in life.

A computer terminal is not some clunky old television with a typewriter in front of it. It is an interface where the mind and body can connect with the universe and move bits of it about.
~ Douglas Adams ~

We may begin to see reality differently simply because the computer ... provides a different angle on reality.
~ Heinz Pagels ~

In today's information-rich society, one almost needs to be a professional researcher. On a daily basis you might need to know batting averages, annual rainfalls, airline timetables, stock histories, or possible names for the new grandchild. In the olden days (B.I. – Before Internet), no one would expect you to have this information at your fingertips – you would have to look it up in the newspaper, check the encyclopedia, or go to the library to get it. Today, most people get their information off the Internet or from CD-ROMs and DVDs, and they get it fast, at lightening speed (or modem speed). We rely on this information not only for business but also for our day-to-day dealings with people as un-business savvy as our grandchildren.

If the computer and the Internet are already as much a part of your existence as your car, phone, and alarm clock, you can give this chapter a quick read-through. But if all this seems like some strange new world to you or your response to the above paragraph was "DV-what's?" then you need to read this chapter carefully, because I suspect that the computer and Internet might not play a large enough (or any) role in your life.

Introduction to the Computer

For those of you not yet in the know, there is a new tool available that is bound to expand your mind, create new synapses in your brain, and add new swear words to your vocabulary. It is called a computer and whether you have accepted it already or not, it is a necessity for a modern Wenjen.

If you don't already own a computer, I'd like you to take a quick quiz.

Please answer the following questions truthfully:

True or False...	**(Circle One)**
I don't think I need a computer in my life.	T or F
I don't need to use a computer to accomplish any of the things I need to do.	T or F
I am too old to learn how to use a computer.	T or F
I can't type, so I'll never be able to use a computer well enough to make it worth the effort.	T or F
I'm not mechanical (I can't even program my VCR!), so I'll never be able to learn how to use a computer!	T or F
A computer is too expensive.	T or F

If you answered true (T) to any of the above – well, you are wrong. Today you would not live without a telephone (can you imagine trying to keep up with your children and grandchildren if you had to rely on their letter-writing habits?!?) or without a car (a complicated piece of machinery with over 18 computers on board). Equally so, you should not be living without a computer. You might not see it yet, but computers can serve you in the same way a telephone and a car can, which you already consider necessities. Computers both speed communication and give you access to a world of goods and information.[1] But if you don't own a computer or haven't spent time online, you probably don't see how this pesky machine could accomplish so much. If the fact that the world has gone and left you behind doesn't motivate you to get one, you may still need a little convincing. So let's look at your objections:

---

[1] The computer can even help you with these two necessities – allowing you to receive your voice mail online or order a car and have it delivered right to your door.

1. I don't think I need a computer in my life. The computer is already in your life. While you weren't looking, a revolution took place in the information and commercial world. Computers and the Internet are now a part of every aspect of American (and international) life, from preschool education to business, banking, leisure. Whether or not you know it, they have already even changed your life by changing the lives of absolutely everyone around you. The computer and the Internet have changed everything in their path. They single-handedly brought America back to the forefront of the economic world. Previously Japan, Southeast Asia, and Germany were considered the wonder countries of economic growth and development. We bought Japanese cars, had our clothes made in Hong Kong, and marveled at German engineering. Americans feared that the Japanese were buying America. Forget about all that now. We are the masters of the new technology and therefore the new economy. Computers, software, and processing chips change and upgrade every six months. Today, only the United States can handle that speed of evolution. Other countries cannot match our pace or ease of change. With our marvelously flexible and inventive minds, and with a country full of people willing to take risks and learn new things, we Americans have left everyone else behind in the proverbial dust. My advice to you would be to join the pace of change as well; otherwise you could spend much of your time reminiscing about the "good old days" without even realizing they are long gone.

2. I don't need to use a computer to accomplish any of the things I need to do. This is utter nonsense. It is the equivalent of saying that there is really nothing you need to accomplish at all. If you do financial transactions (and who doesn't), if you travel, if you read the news, if you pay your taxes, if you need information about your health (or any other matter under the sun), if you want to order prescriptions, if you want to buy or sell anything, if you write anything, or if you merely want to "stay in touch" with someone, then you need a computer to do it. "Need?" you say? "I don't *need* a computer to do these things." Well, you also don't really *need* your car to get things done (there is the bus after all) or your phone to keep in touch with the world (there is the mail). But just as a car and a phone help you to function with ease in the modern world, so too can a computer. Every aspect of life is now managed, referenced, researched, written, and influenced by the computer. If you want to stay in contact with the rest of the world, you need a computer. It has become a basic tool of life in our society.

3. I am too old to learn how to use a computer. You may be too old to climb Mount Everest, but you are never too old to learn something new – especially something as easy as this. I regularly teach four-year-olds how to use the computer. Four-year-olds! And my "oldest" student was an 80-year-old man who wanted to connect with his great-grandson online.

4. I can't type, so I'll never be able to use a computer well enough to make it worth the effort. Well, the mouse helps a lot. Also, a lot of people in the world can't type well either, and so most good computer programs require very little typing (unless of course they are word processing programs). For the most part, hunting and pecking will get you by just fine. However, if you decide you want to speed up your keyboard time, there are many good computer programs that will teach you how to type in no time at all.[2]

For those of you who want to eliminate typing from your computer experience entirely or who need to do word processing and can't stand to hunt and peck, there are also some excellent voice-recognition programs that can allow you to dictate straight into the computer. By all accounts, these work fairly well, with no need to pause between words or to speak in a stilted fashion.[3]

5. I am not mechanical, so I'll never be able to learn how to use a computer. We're talking about being able to e-mail someone! Although a computer is a complex piece of machinery, rest assured you will never need to program one. If you simply focus on the programs you need to accomplish your task, you can master a computer rather quickly. Also, the wonderful thing about computers is that the programs designed for it are so easy to use. Programmers and software designers deliberately write their software for us – the regular people. As a result, their idea of a successful program is one that is useful – and as intuitively

---

[2] Mavis Beacon teaches typing and can be found online at www.mavisbeacon.com.

[3] Dragon's Naturally Speaking Preferred, L&H's Voice Xpress Professional, and Philips Free Speech 2000 are all superlative programs.

obvious as possible – to you, the regular person who doesn't have the time, interest, or ability to master another tool.

Finally, I'd like to make a quick pitch for the IDG book series, entitled "Teach Yourself ... [Quicken, Microsoft Word, etc.]" and the "Que... " book series. I use these books as teaching aids and recommend them highly. They are wonderful because they are constructed to teach *visually*, which is exactly the way computer programs are designed to be used. IDG's instruction methods are the perfect match for anyone wanting to learn a computer quickly and intuitively.

6. A computer is too expensive. Oh please – you are affluent, which means you can (and should) spend money on things that are important; and the computer will be very important in your Kaneka and in your future Wenjen life. Eventually, you will find it as important to you as your car and phone – and you wouldn't dream of not spending money on them would you?

Furthermore, the cost of a good PC (personal computer) with a printer is constantly coming down. The cost of a Macintosh with printer is about 25% higher then an IBM compatible. You can go up from there if you decide you want additional components, but if you are just starting out, a basic computer is good enough for now. Given how fast computers upgrade and change, by the time you wish you had purchased a fancier feature, the feature will have been improved several times over since you bought your system. If instead you wait to add components until just when you are ready to use them, you can guarantee that you will always get the best and newest features on the market.

If I don't know anything about computers, how do I know what kind to buy?

A fortunate consequence of waiting so long to buy your first computer is that by now almost every basic computer system on the market comes with everything you need to begin working on programs (don't worry, it's easy).

There are two major computer types – Macintoshes (made by Apple Computers) and PCs made by pretty much everyone else. A year ago I would have said, "Don't buy a Macintosh." But now with the new I-Macs, Apple has undergone a Kaneka. In general, more software is available for the PC, but the I-Mac is easier to use, is an all-around great machine, and comes in your favorite color (as opposed to the bland beige all PCs seem to come in). The only remaining concerns are the following:

1. *Macs can read both Mac- and PC-formatted floppy disks, but PCs can only read PC-formatted disks.* This is only of real importance if someone you want to share hard files with, like your partner or a family member, already uses one or the other type of computer. This might influence your choice of computers, but you can also easily make this a non-issue by purchasing the translation software and installing it on the PC.

2. *Some of the new Macs come with a built-in modem, CD drive, and DVD player but don't have built-in drive for 3.5" floppy disks.* The time is coming when these disks won't be used any longer, but unfortunately that time is not now. Mac got a bit ahead of itself by excluding this feature. So if you do buy a Mac, just make sure to include an external drive for the 3.5" floppy drive in your package (it is small, comes in a matching color, and plugs easily into the main computer).

Outside these issues, the kind of computer you go with is entirely a matter of preference.

And Software?

Once you get a computer, I would recommend acquiring additional software in the following areas:

Word processing: Most likely, your computer came with a word processing program already installed. However, if the program is not Microsoft Word, I would suggest purchasing it and using it instead. It is not that I am a huge Microsoft fan, but these days almost everyone, regardless of whether they use a Mac or a PC, uses Microsoft Word as their program of choice. So get it. It is simple, will allow you to be compatible with almost anyone else you share files with, and will offer you more writing features than you will ever need.

Financial: This will help you budget and keep track of where you spend your money. It can also help you with your investments, taxes, and any other financial things you do. The two best programs I have found are Quicken and Microsoft Money. I have used Quicken for about ten years, and I am now a whiz at overspending my budget. Using online

banking and bill paying in conjunction with one of these programs is
another real time-saver and helps make overall financial management
much easier.[4]

Digital Photography and Archived Photo Albums: Manipulating
and displaying one's pictures on the computer has become an easy and
popular pastime. Digital cameras have come of age for all but the most
professional photographer; digital video cameras commonly offer a
"still" option to take digital snapshots; and standard Kodak processing
for regular 35mm film now includes printing onto a 3.5" floppy disk or
CD-ROM. You will even find this new feature at the photo counter of
your local grocery or drugstore. The nice thing about the digital world
is that basic photo imaging software usually comes free with your new
camera or Kodak photo CD or disk. But there are many programs you
can purchase in order to manipulate and design your photographs and
photo displays.

Once in the computer, it is easy to manipulate your photos –
eliminating red eye, putting Fido's head on the cat, or having any amount
of "artistic" fun. You can create cards, posters, postcards – even digital
photo albums that can be posted online for everyone to see. Or simply e-
mail your photos directly to family and friends. You can send your
grandchildren the one of you standing on top of Mount McKinley in
Alaska to show them that grandpa is not a wuss.

The Internet

All of these activities represent important uses of the computer.
However, one phenomenon has created a new world of information and
commerce and revolutionizes a different industry every day. That is the
Internet – a group of computers (no one knows how many) all linked
together to talk to each other and share information around the world.

So why do *you* need the Internet? Our world has grown quite
complex. No longer is there just one airfare from Los Angeles to New
York. Hotels don't have a common price. The monsoons in India affect
the price of bread in New York. There are new health findings by the
hour (though scientists still haven't found that chocolate is good for you).

---

[4] See Chapter 12 for more information on this topic.

On the Internet you can get information on all of the above; make air, hotel, and rental car reservations; and buy almost anything you want (and many things you don't need). You can bid at auctions from such diverse companies as eBay (I bought an antique camera) and Sotheby's (there I just enjoy viewing the art). You can learn history directly from the Smithsonian Institution or get your news delivered daily to your e-mail by the *New York Times* – for free! Nowadays, one cannot drive past a billboard or watch a television commercial without seeing "www" (World Wide Web). That is because the World Wide Web provides an astounding, astronomical, and overwhelming amount of knowledge, services, and information. And though what is available now represents only a small fraction of what will be available in even the near future, the Internet has already revolutionized the way ideas are learned, utilized, and shared. The Internet is a resource, a tool, a store, and an adventure.

Many good books can help you learn how to use the Internet (again, check out the "Teach Yourself..." IDG book series and the "Que..." book series). My only aim is to acquaint you with some of the Internet's basic functions so that you can feel confident getting started.

Servers and Service Providers: AOL, Earthlink, et al.

In order to get "logged on" to the Internet you will need a way of connecting your computer to that huge network of other computers. There are several different methods of doing this, but by far the most common is through your household phone line. To connect your computer to your phone line you will need to acquire and install software from an "Internet Service Provider." This provider will give you all the requisite software to start you out surfing the Web and receiving e-mail; it'll give you a local dial-up number for your computer modem to dial into, and a user name, which you can use as your e-mail address. Two of the most frequently used Internet providers are AOL (America Online) and Earthlink. They are both excellent providers with a good interface (translation: they are easy to personalize and negotiate). They have seamless entry to your e-mail. They have initial start-up pages ("homepages") that can be easily personalized to include up-to-date information on whatever is important to you, such as your stock portfolio, local weather, and news. Their homepages also have links to the most popular search engines as well as to major Internet shopping centers, such as Amazon, eToys, and eBay.

E-mail

A wonderful invention. Almost everyone that uses it loves it. Just don't give out your e-mail address to too many companies unless you want to get bombarded with "spam" (good old-fashioned junk mail). However, companies can send such useful information as travel specials, new gadgets, or events that are only available online. E-mail also makes keeping in touch with old friends, new friends, and maybe even relatives a fabulously simple enterprise, and e-mail directories and search engines make finding their e-mail addresses online even simpler.

Online Communities and User Groups

One of the many benefits of the Internet is the ability to contact people all over the world. As a cybersurfer (yes, it does sound cool), you may now enter virtual communities (called chat groups or bulletin boards) to exchange ideas with painters, writers, people traveling to Southeast Asia, or even other bridge aficionados.

Gone are the days when seniors used to say, "It would be nice to have young people around." Today, with the Internet, seniors can commune with young people, old people, or people of any age. Although you may have some aches and pains in common with other 50+ individuals, a person in a virtual community shows no age, and by reading and following the ideas in this book, you will soon have a lot to talk about to virtual individuals of all ages.

Search Engines

These are programs that read all the millions of pages of information on the Internet and help you to extract only those that you need. Most home pages will offer you a selection of search engines from which to choose. Which one you use depends on the information you want and the style of inquiry you like. I find that www.askjeeves.com is one of the easiest to use as it lets you phrase your question in regular English. Other search engines are Yahoo, Alta Vista, the Mining Company, and Lycos. As you learn more about the Internet your searches will probably become more specific and you might eventually find that different search engines serve your needs better.

Another search option is using an online directory. AOL, Earthlink, and Yahoo all have good ones. These directories narrow down topics from the general to specific so that you may click through pages, much like looking through an index of a book, to find your needed information. Just as useful as a search engine, these will often lead you directly to the most popular sites on your topic.

Amazon.com and B&N.com

For those who read, ordering books online is a tremendous treat. Still, many offline book buyers can't imagine giving up the experience of thumbing through actual books in a brick and mortar store to get an idea of what to read. What you'll gain if you shop Amazon and Barnes and Noble Online are reviews and buying comparisons.

If you look up a book on either of these sites you will usually find ratings and reviews by other customers who have already purchased and read the book you are considering. These ratings and reviews offer insights way beyond the five minutes of mere page thumbing. Furthermore, you'll find the buying preferences of the customers who bought the book you are considering. This way it easy to see whether "your type" of people are reading the book in question, or what other books they have read that you might be interested in reading as well. This is not to say that you have to spend all your book-buying time online, but as a research tool for new books, these sites can be invaluable.

Summing Up

I may sound over-enthusiastic about the computer, but I have seen many children's, adults', and seniors' lives changed by this new addition to their family. To engender this momentous transformation in your own life, I would suggest doing the following:

1. Accept that a computer with Internet access is a necessity in both your Kaneka and your future Wenjen life.
2. If you don't already have one, get on the stick and get yourself a basic computer package.
3. Purchase word processing and financial software.
4. Contact an Internet Service Provider and sign up. The company will send you all the software you need to get online.

5. Purchase a few good books on basic computer and Internet use – and get a move on! There is literally a whole new world waiting for you out there.

Today it is not what you know, but what information you
can research.
~ Unknown ~

There is a new form of information and communication our there, and it is the Internet. If you don't use the telephone, drive a car, or watch television then you can ignore it. Otherwise consider it part of a communication revolution. It is growing faster then television did in its heyday and the effect will probably be greater then the Industrial revolution. It is helping to tear apart the Bamboo curtain and lifting the veils of the Middle East. It can entertain you, make you think, and provide information. It has invaded the classroom and the world of business.

The Internet is both easy and complex. It you know what you are looking for you can probably find it, although it may take you some time.   If you have an address (domain name) life becomes easy.

This chapter gives you a list of some of the best address for various topics, such as seniors, travel, financial etc.   There are constantly new ones appearing and many magazines will list and write about new websites.   You can make note of these and add them to your list of favorites.

Use this list to start you research and your launching into a new information age.

Internet sites for the Active-Retiree

Art, Music, Literature
http://www.prs.net/midi.html
More than 7,000 classical music files in MIDI format from more than 500 composers. An integrated search engine makes for fugue-finding with finesse.

http://www.literature.org/Works
The full text of everything from Aesop to Voltaire.

http://www.hart.bbk.ac.uk/VirtualLibrary.html
Comprehensive listing of links to collections, exhibitions, museums, universities, online teaching resources, art history organizations and online publications.

http://www.jazzonln.com
The world's first commercial interactive network devoted to jazz. All styles are covered.

http://www.paris.org/Musees/Louvre
A virtual tour with links to the treasures of the Louvre.

http://www.pastperfect.com
The sounds of the 20s, 30s and 40s, all digitally remastered and available on CD-ROM. Lots of sound samples and photos in the Photo Archive section.

Auctions
www.ebay.com
Over 4,5 mil. items. Also, eBay's buyers and sellers are a mostly honorable lot.

http://auctions.yahoo.com/
Well stocked, but less lively community as in eBay.

Computers and electronics
www.necx.com
30,000 products plus tracking the mfg rebates.

www.outpost.com
300 different cameras and fair prices.

www.etown.com
Electronics, 5000 items and product reviews

Computer Goods
www.cdw.com
The largest collection of CD's and DVD's. 500,000 titles and 70,000 songs that can be digitally downloaded.

www.pcconnection.com
Both offer good selection and low prices and also tech support for the products they sell. Also, PC Connection offer low overnight shipping fees and super-fast delivery (same day)

Computer Software
www.buy.com
8200 software products and price guarantee.

Financial
www.quicken.com
Investments, mortgages, taxes and retirement planning.

www.quotesmith.com
Life insurance quotes from hundreds of companies.

Health Care
www.mayohealth.org
Good articles and research information.

www.onhealth.com
A database of more then 350 disease. Easy to use.

www.healthgrades.com
Referrals for doctors. Over 600,000physicians.

www.planetRX.com
Best service and prices for most prescription drugs.

Learning and creativity
www.lcweb.loc.gov
The library of Congress

www.si.edu
Smithsonian Institution

www.discovery.com
If you like the Discovery Channel then this is a natural.

Lifestyle
www.homegrocer.com
Food delivered to your door. The jury is still out on this one.

www.cookinglight.com
For health meals to enjoy your Kaneka.

www.operabase.com
All about opera.

News and Sports
www.sportingnews.com
Timely, comprehensive reporting.

www.pbs.org
If you love PBS this is worth a look.

www.CNN.com
The best online news source. The New York Times is a close second.

www.ESPN.com
The best sport site for all around sports.

Living Abroad
www.aca.ch
American citizens abroad. Voting rights, etc.

www.aaro-intl.org
American residents overseas.
Medicare and Census.

www.liveabroad.com
Personalized reports, pro's and cons of living in certain countries.

Search engines
www.alltheweb.com
Uncover links that other engines overlook.

www.google.com
Uncanny accuracy, has an extra search button that takes you to the
one site most pertinent to your query.

ww.hotbot.com
Fast accurate searches that deliver relevance ranked results.

http://magellan.excite.com
People Finder accessed through a special interface that makes it easier
to use.

Sports Active
www.crossroadscycling.com
Wonderful bike trips by a well organized group that pays lots of
attention to details.

www.elderhostel.org
Elderhostel - A great collection of educational adventures trips all
over the world for people who believe learning is a lifelong process.

www.bikevt.com
Bike Vermont - A wonderful group of inn to inn biking and hiking
trips from a company that's been doing it for 24 years.

www.butterfield.com
Butterfield & Robinson - A luxury biking or hiking trip by a company
whose motto is "slow down and see the world".

www.skiersover50.com
Over the Hill Gang - The worlds premier group for well season skiers. At least 30 ski trips annually and a number of summer adventures.

www.countrywalkers.com
Country Walkers - Wonderful walking tours for those that like to have all the comforts at the end of their walks.

Sporting Goods
www.fogdog.com
Great Lacross sticks and almost everything else to start you on your new sports path.

Stocks
www.techstocks.com
Silicon Investor gives information about high-tech stocks.

www.ragingbull.com
Raging Bull is chatting about stocks.

www.schwab.com
The largest on-line brokerage. Excellent service, especially if you become a platinum customer.

Travel
www.expedia.com
Buy tickets, reserve a car, line up a hotel room.

www.travelocity.com
Personalized guides and airline seat maps.

www.Gorp.com
If you are planning an outdoor trip this site is a must.

www.biztravel.com
Useful for upgrading and finding hotels with all the business amenities.

www.americanexpress.com
All types of travel information and some great deals, especially if you have a platinum card.

www.ticketplanet.com
If an around-the-world-trip is on your "Big List" then this site is for you.

www.holidayfestival.com
All the festivals to see or avoid around the world.

www.im.aa.com
American Airlines special site with discount fares for seniors. Go to *"Specials"* and then to *"Senior Fares"*

www.silverwingsplus.com
United Airlines special site with discount fares for seniors.

www.haystack-mtn.org
A place to develop skills and nurture the creative spirit. A unique campus in a stunning natural setting. Classes in Blacksmithing, Clay pottery, Metal working, Wood sculpturing and many more.

<u>Internal Journey</u>
www.newagetravel.com
Organize trips to explore your self and the world.

www.healthytravel.com
Great privately designed tours.

www.retreatsonline.com
Is a listing for all sorts of retreats. Also, you can check:
www.retreatsonline.com/guide/wilderness.htm
for a comprehensive listing of wilderness retreats in US and Canada.

www.monitor.net/~circle/vision.htm
Workshops and retreats with Native American practice.

www.hoffmaninstitute.org
A good personal development and spiritual retreat, with well-trained people and spas in natural settings.

www.yogasite.com
A place to research a yoga style.

Wine and Gourmet Food

www.wine.com
For the perfect merlot or 2,500 other labels.

www.rarewine.com
The domain name says it all. Only if you really love wines and want to spend money.

www.tavolo.com
Pretty much anything, including a $2,000 tub of caviar.

Books that cover aspects of Active-Retirement

Financial Planning

The Wall Street Journal Guide to Planning Your Financial Future :
The Easy-To-Read Guide to Planning for Retirement
by Alan M. Siegel, Virginia B. Morris, Kenneth M. Morris

Live Rich : Everything You Need to Know to Be Your Own Boss,
Whoever You Work for
by Mark Levine, Stephen M. Pollan

Die Broke : A Radical, Four-Part Financial Plan
by Mark Levine, Stephen M. Pollan (Introduction)

You've Earned It, Don't Lose It: Mistakes You Can't Afford to Make
When You Retire
by Suze Orman (Introduction), Linda Mead (Contributor)

Journaling

Your Life As Story: Discovering the 'New Autobiography' and Writing
Memoir As Literature
by Tristine Rainer

The Artist's Way: A Spiritual Path to Higher Creativity
by Julia Cameron

Travel and other locations

Dynamic Travel - Thrilling Trips For Your Golden Years
by George Hawley, Jack O'Hara (Illustrator)

*The Psychology of Retirement: How to Cope Successfully with a
Major Life Transition*
by The Everyday Psychologist

Volunteer Opportunities for Seniors Away from Home
by Lewis D. Solomon

*America's 100 Best Places to Retire: The Only Guide You Need to
Today's Top Retirement Towns*
by Richard L. Fox (Editor)

*The Complete Guide to Second Homes for Vacation, Retirement, and
Investment*
by Gary W. Eldred

*Unbelievable Good Deals and Great Adventures That You Absolutely
Can't Get Unless You're over 50*
by Joan Rattner Heilman (April 1999)

Computers

Mr. Modem's Internet Guide for Seniors (Internet)
by Richard A. Sherman

300 Incredible Things for Seniors on the Internet
by Joe West, Ken Leebow

Index

I

For information about inviting Peter Silton to speak to an

organization or event, please contact:

N.P. Financials
P.O. Box 49891
Los Angeles, CA 90049 U.S.A.
Phone-FAX: (310) 471-1353
e-Mail npfinancial@earthlink.net

ORDER FORM

N.P. Financials

P.O. Box 49891
Los Angeles, CA 90049 U.S.A.
Phone-FAX: (310) 471-1353
e-Mail npfinancial@earthlink.net

Please send me the following:

QUANTITY		AMOUNT
_____	Active-Retirement for Affluent Workaholics $19.95	_____

Total for books _____

Sales tax for CA orders 8.25% _____

Shipping $3.50 first copy($1.50 per additional copy) _____

Total amount enclosed (US Dollars) _____

ACTIVE-RETIRED NEWSLETTER

New information about special senior fares, travel, and Internet sites with special interest to seniors.

Quarterly: Printed version $49.50 per year.
E-mail (confidential) $39.50 per year

Name: _____

Address: _____

City: _____ State: _____ Zip: _____

Books _____ Free copy of Newsletter _____ Subscription P_ _E_

E-Mail address _____ (List will not be sold)